THE ANATOMY OF THE PERFECT WEBSITE

Inside Google's Training Guide:
How To Turn It Into A Site That
Wins Customers and Search Rankings

Rafael Romis

Paperback ISBN: 979-8-218-67259-1

eBook ISBN: 979-8-218-67272-0

DEDICATION

To my father—who taught me how business really works, long before I ever built one.

To the visionaries chasing Apple's aesthetic without Apple's context.

And to the *"I just need something super simple"* crowd, who haven't realized yet that intentional simplicity is the hardest thing to get right.

This is for you.

Read this before your next redesign.

TABLE OF CONTENTS

Foreword

If there's one mistake I see over and over again, it's this: Business owners treat their website like a piece of art, not like a business asset.

They obsess over the visuals. They debate fonts. They tinker with animations. And they pour hours, sometimes months, into a website that looks great but doesn't actually do anything.

No strategy. No structure. No measurable goals. Just vibes.

That's why I wrote this book.

This book is for every founder, business owner, and marketing leader who knows their website could be doing more—but isn't sure where to start.

It's for those in the early stages, before the first draft of the homepage is even mocked up. It's for those with a website that "works," but doesn't convert. And it's especially for those who are about to spend a chunk of their marketing budget on a redesign, without a clear sense of what they actually need.

In an ideal world, every business owner would read this book before they built their site.

Because once you understand how a website should be built—what it's actually supposed to do—everything else becomes clearer. Your messaging sharpens. Your navigation gets cleaner. Your conversions go up. Your trust signals align. And you stop trying to reinvent the wheel every few years.

Think of this book as a user experience framework, a masterclass in SEO, and a blueprint for better business thinking—all in one.

And if you're wondering how all this ties into search rankings, it's not by coincidence. Google's own Search Quality Rater Guidelines (the document used to train their human evaluators) are based on the same core principles: clarity, purpose, trust, and helpfulness.

Throughout this book, we'll reference those guidelines and show you exactly how to apply them in ways that don't just improve rankings—they improve the user experience for your real visitors, too.

At its core, this isn't just a book about websites. It's a book about how great businesses communicate. It's about clarity, purpose, empathy, and momentum.

It just so happens that the medium we're applying it to is digital.

The principles you'll find in the following pages apply just as well to brick-and-mortar stores, consulting practices, or even physical showrooms. Because great businesses do one thing really well: They make it incredibly easy for the right people to say yes.

They remove confusion.
They anticipate questions.
They eliminate friction.
They build trust.

And they do it all without ever feeling pushy or complicated.

That's what the best websites do, too. They're not just digital brochures. They're your digital front desk. Your first handshake. Your pitch. Your sales rep. Your customer support assistant. And your most scalable tool for growth... if you use it right.

Let me tell you a quick story.

About twelve years ago, when I started Weberous, my web design agency, we were still trying to land our first few clients. We came up with what we thought was a brilliant idea: we'd offer to design a full homepage for free, with zero commitment. Just a sample. A no-risk offer to prove what we could do.

We built an elaborate sales page to pitch it. Animations, long-form copy, every bell and whistle we could cram in, so we can show off what we can do. Then we launched the ads.

1% conversion. We were stunned.

We were offering free homepage designs—no strings attached—and 99% of people looking for web design said "no thanks." Our landing page was gorgeous. I wish I could pull it up so I can add a screenshot here, but imagine an air balloon that would float around the page as you scroll, parallax effects, and the whole enchilada.

That's 12 years ago, when those things were all the rage. But it somehow missed the spot.

So we trimmed the page. Cut the fluff. Tightened the message. Suddenly, we were converting at 3%. Triple the results, just by simplifying.

Eventually, we landed on a version that was just one screen. A strong headline on the left, a short explanation underneath, a call to action, and a one-minute video on the right explaining how it worked.

That version converted at 7%. **We had to pause the ads just to keep up with the leads**.

That experience taught me something I've seen play out again and again:

Clarity beats clever. Simplicity beats spectacle. Intent beats aesthetics.

This book will show you how to do exactly that.

Not just how to make a beautiful website, but how to make one that actually works. One that's built to serve your business, your audience, and your goals.

I've built hundreds of websites, from small startups to global brands, and I've seen what works (and what absolutely doesn't). What's inside this book is everything I've learned from that journey.

It's not theoretical. It's not fluffy. It's built from real work, real data, and real results.

Whether you're building your first website or your fifteenth, I promise you: what's inside this book will help you build better.

Not just a prettier website.

A **perfect** one—because it's perfect for your business, your audience, and your goals.

Let's get started.

— Rafael Romis

Introduction:
What Makes a Website "Perfect"?

A perfect website isn't about trends or aesthetics alone. It's about achieving your specific goals while delivering an exceptional user experience.

The best websites guide visitors seamlessly through their journey.

They remove confusion, build trust, and lead people toward action without ever feeling pushy or forced. Whether that action is a purchase, a form submission, or simply building brand awareness, the website is doing its job and doing it well.

In this book, we'll break down every component of a well-structured, high-performing website.

We'll look at how to align your site's structure with your business goals, how to create intuitive user experiences that keep visitors engaged, and how to ensure your site is optimized for both users and search engines—because those two things are no longer separate goals.

In fact, nearly everything covered in this book is aligned with the principles shared by Google.

While the interpretations and recommendations presented here are based on my own analysis and do not represent official statements or endorsements by Google, you will see that the connection is clear.

Years ago, an internal "Search Quality Rater Guidelines" (SQRG) document (meant for Google's manual reviewers) was leaked, giving the world a rare look into the specific criteria used to assess a site's quality.

And while algorithms have evolved since then, the principles haven't changed.

Today, Google actually makes these detailed guidelines publicly available.

It's fascinating how much Google's expectations now mirror those of real users. In 2025, there's practically no difference between building for people and building for search engines.

If you design your website to serve your visitors well—clear structure, valuable content, fast performance, trustworthy signals—Google will reward you for it.

And that's not an accident.

With over 8.5 billion searches per day, Google has access to more behavioral data than any other company on the planet.

They know what people want.

Their ranking algorithms are powered by how users actually behave, what they click on, how long they stay, whether they bounce, and whether they find what they were looking for.

So when Google favors a site, it's because the data says people do too.

That's also why you'll notice that many of the best websites—across industries, business types, and goals—often follow a surprisingly similar structure.

Not because they're copying each other, but because they're built around how humans think, browse, and make decisions.

We all process online content in relatively predictable ways. That's why certain layouts consistently outperform others.

You could go to one of the big website theme stores (like the Shopify Theme Store for eCommerce or ThemeForest for everything else), sort by best selling, and find templates that are likely to perform.

And yes—if you're in a rush, you could just use one of them.

But that would be like buying a suit off the rack. It might look fine. It might even be close enough. But if you want it to truly fit—to reflect your brand, your audience, your goals—you'll need to tailor it.

And unlike a suit, your website is constantly evolving.

Your business grows, your audience shifts, your products change.

The real value isn't in just copying what works—it's in understanding *why* it works. Because when you understand that, you won't just build a better website today. You'll know how to keep improving it tomorrow.

And that's the core idea behind this book: build your website the right way for your audience, and everything else—SEO, conversion rates, trust, and growth—starts to fall into place.

Let's get into it.

Chapter 1:
A Website's True Purpose

Why Purpose Drives Everything

Most websites suck. It's because most businesses approach their website backwards. They start with colors. Fonts. Layouts. Fancy effects. Maybe a trendy design they saw on a competitor's site or even a popular template. The result? A pretty website that doesn't actually do anything for the business.

At best it looks great, but what's the point of that?

Here's the truth: a great website isn't one that looks good—it's one that performs.

The perfect website is built with purpose. Because it's "the perfect website" for that specific purpose. *The keyword here is specific.*

This focus on purpose isn't just good business sense; it directly mirrors how Google evaluates website quality. This isn't a guess. It's in Google's own documentation: their Search Quality Rater Guidelines (SQRG) require evaluators to assess whether a page fulfills its purpose. That's a core component of what they call a Page Quality (PQ) rating.

So, purpose-first design isn't just good UX—it's good SEO.

You don't want a vague "we want to grow" or "it's time for a redesign" kind of purpose, but a specific, measurable goal: generating qualified leads, selling products, onboarding new clients, educating visitors, reducing support tickets, or something else entirely.

That goal becomes the lens through which every design, piece of content, or even technical decision is made.

Think of your website like a machine.

You don't start assembling a machine by polishing the outside. You start by knowing exactly what it's supposed to do. You build it in order to do that one thing as efficiently as it can.

If your website doesn't have a clear job, it won't perform well—no matter how nice it looks.

This applies whether you're a solo consultant or a billion-dollar enterprise. In fact, the bigger the business, the more dangerous it is to skip this step. You'll end up with a bloated site that tries to serve too many masters, and ends up serving none.

This chapter is about defining that "goal", your website's true purpose, and building everything else focused around that.

We'll start by looking at the four most common website goals and how each one changes the structure and strategy of your site.

Then we'll explore how understanding your visitors' intent, and the stage they're in on their journey, should shape your content and layout.

We'll look at a real-world case study where a lack of clarity in purpose led to a bloated, ineffective site, and how fixing it transformed the experience and results.

And finally, we'll close this chapter with a focused action plan so you can define your site's purpose clearly and confidently.

The Core Website Goals

Not five goals. One goal.

That goal is your website's primary job—the one outcome that matters most. It's the reason the site exists in the first place. And until you define it clearly, everything else you build is just guesswork.

So what are we talking about when we say "goal"?

A real goal is something specific and measurable. Something that informs every design choice, every piece of copy, and every page on your site.

We're not talking about "having a presence online" or "getting our brand out there." These are not goals.

Ask yourself *why* you want those. That will help you figure out the actual goal—and that should always be your first step.

A website without a real goal is like hiring a salesperson who doesn't know what they're supposed to sell.

Let's break down the most common types.

Direct Sales (Ecommerce)

If you're running an online store, your goal is obvious: make sales.

In most cases, that means fast, mobile-first performance, smart shoppable navigation, great product photography and copy, an easy checkout with as few steps as possible, and strong trust signals like reviews, guarantees, and return policies.

But not always. You have to consider the product and your specific audience. How do they buy?

A common mistake here is focusing too much on the brand and not enough on the experience.

Sure, you want a beautiful homepage—but if it takes five clicks to get to the actual products, you're bleeding conversions.

The goal isn't to impress: it's to sell.

Lead Generation

Lead generation is the most common goal for service businesses, consultants, agencies, and B2B companies in general.

Your website's job is to get someone to reach out, and that comes in many different forms. It could be to schedule a call, request a quote, book a demo, or fill out a contact form.

To support that, everything on your site needs to build trust and remove friction.

Think about what your clients tell you when you talk to them, then make sure you address that directly on your site. That means clear, benefit-driven copy, proof of expertise (like case studies, testimonials, and recognizable clients), and simple, well-placed forms and calls to action.

No fluff. No filler. No rabbit holes.

A common mistake here is trying to act like an eCommerce site. You're not selling a product on the spot, so don't overwhelm people with feature lists and pricing tables on your homepage, unless that's truly your main selling point.

Your job is to start the conversation, not to close the deal.

Brand Awareness & Thought Leadership

This one's a little softer, but still important especially for founders, influencers, or consultants. The goal here is to build authority, grow an audience, and be seen as the go-to expert in your space.

Notice the subtle difference between lead generation and brand awareness. Here, you're not trying to get them to reach out. You want them to trust you and your expertise. Pushing them toward making contact too soon could actually backfire.

If this is your goal, your website should highlight your best content up front—whether that's blog posts, videos, podcasts, or interviews.

It should make it easy for people to subscribe, follow, or stay in touch. You should showcase your credibility: speaking gigs, media appearances, credentials. And you need to create a narrative that's clearly "you."

The most common mistake? Too much "about me" fluff.

People don't care that much about you—they care about themselves. So cut to the chase and give them content that helps *them* and *their* brands.

Customer Support & Retention

This is common for SaaS and membership sites, and it should be treated differently from their lead generation websites.

The goal isn't just to attract new customers—it's to serve existing ones better. That means your site should:

- Make it easy for users to find help through a knowledge base, FAQ, or live chat.
- Allow customers to access their accounts, billing info, or training.
- Keep users up to date with new features and product announcements.

A common mistake here is treating the website as just a marketing tool. If your current customers are the ones using your site most, but the content is all "salesy," then you're doing it wrong.

The site should be all about support and nurturing, not pushing people toward a purchase they've already made.

Figure 1. The core website goals.

The table below outlines key elements that support the four major website goals. Use it as a guide to understand the differences and prioritize the right features based on what your site needs to achieve.

Direct Sales (Ecommerce)	Lead Generation (Services/B2B)	Brand Awareness / Thought Leadership	Customer Support / Retention
High-quality product photos/videos	Clear descriptions of services & outcomes	High-quality blog posts/ articles	Searchable Knowledge Base / FAQs
Detailed, benefit-focused descriptions	Benefit-driven headlines & copy	Videos / Podcast episodes	User account portal (login, history)
Customer reviews & ratings	Case studies & specific results	Company story / About Us page	Billing information access
Clear pricing, shipping, & return policies	Testimonials & client logos	Founder/Team bios	How-to guides / Tutorials
Easy site navigation & product search	Simple contact/quote/demo forms	Speaking gigs / Media mentions	Product update announcements
Streamlined multi-step checkout	Clear calls-to-action	Credentials / Certifications	Community forum access
Security badges/ guarantees	Lead magnets (guides, webinars)	Easy email subscribe / follow options	Clear support contact channels

Choosing Your Primary Goal

Now here's where a lot of businesses go sideways: they try to do everything at once.

They want to sell, generate leads, build authority, and support their existing customers... all on the homepage.

The result? A bloated mess. Conflicting CTAs. Mixed messages. A homepage that's trying to talk to four different people at the same time.

This is more common than you'd think.

Here's the fix: pick your primary goal—the one thing that matters most. Then structure the entire site around that.

Yes, you can support multiple goals on subpages. In fact, you should. But your homepage, and most of your navigation, should be laser-focused on your primary.

Think of it like this: If a first-time visitor lands on your homepage, what's the one thing you most want them to end up doing?

That's your primary goal.

And if you do it right, that's the backbone of everything else that follows.

Now, before you start thinking that there's a single best-practice playbook for this—there isn't. There are always exceptions. But there are no exceptions to the rule.

The rule is that *you have to build for your specific goal and audience*. That's why it all starts by defining these.

For example, we built a website for a very high-end luggage brand and their main goal was to sell. For them, it wasn't about simplicity or rushing to the sale. We had to intrigue and warm up their customers, in order to eventually lead to a sale. They had to be nurtured.

Their homepage was very interactive—it had visitors scrolling through it to learn about the different features and quality of craftsmanship behind their core product.

This worked great for them, even though it would go against best practices for many other stores.

Remember, don't assume that a certain type of website is great for your business just because it works well for a different business. I see this all the time with Shopify stores.

Just don't assume, and try to avoid getting "inspired" by other websites, particularly industry leading ones.

Let's just say that If I had a dime for every time a new client told us that they want their website to look like Apple, then I'd have a ton of dimes.

Once you've identified your website's primary goal, the next step is to think about the specific information, content, and features ('assets') needed to achieve it effectively. This table shows typical assets associated with each goal. Every case is different, so they're not set in stone. I'm just sharing them for guidance. Use this to brainstorm the specific assets you need to create/highlight on your site to guide visitors towards your primary goal.

Understanding Visitor Intent: The Key to Conversions

A website is only effective if it aligns with the needs and expectations of its visitors.

That means understanding visitor intent—why someone is on your website in the first place, and what they're hoping to do once they arrive.

There are three primary types of intent: informational, commercial, and transactional.

- **Informational intent** is when someone is in research mode. They're looking for general knowledge, education, or guidance, but not necessarily with the goal of buying or taking action right now.
- **Commercial intent** is when someone is investigating options. They're not just learning. They're actively evaluating potential solutions, providers, or products in preparation for a future decision.
- **Transactional intent** means the visitor is ready to act. They know what they want and they're looking to do it now—whether it's to buy, schedule, sign up, or get in touch.

To help clarify the differences between these, let's look at how these play out through a familiar lens: *Google search behavior*.

Most people's journeys start on Google, so understanding the types of searches that align with each level of intent can help us plan a website that mirrors that journey.

For example, someone searching *how to market a small business* is demonstrating informational intent—they're trying to learn the basics and aren't yet looking to hire an agency. A person who types in *best marketing agencies in Los Angeles* is showing commercial intent, actively comparing providers. And a search like *hire digital marketing agency near me* reflects transactional intent, signaling they're ready to make a decision and take action.

Your website needs to account for all three stages, especially if your goal is to convert a higher percentage of visitors.

If your entire site only speaks to transactional visitors—people ready to buy now—you're likely losing out on the broader audience that's still in research or comparison mode.

Likewise, many businesses make the mistake of filling their homepage with general content that speaks to everyone at once. The result is just confusing, because of conflicting calls to action, and no clear next step for the user.

A better approach is to think in terms of pathways.

For example, your homepage should primarily speak to commercial-intent visitors—those evaluating options—because that's the most common mindset of a first-time visitor. From there, you can guide high-intent visitors directly to conversion pages, and direct low-intent visitors to more educational content that builds trust.

In a recent project for a law firm, we ran into a common mismatch between audience intent and site structure. The firm was driving most of its traffic through paid ads, targeting keywords that showed strong transactional intent—in their case it say *hire immigration attorney*. These were visitors looking to take action immediately.

But the ads landed on their homepage, which was full of long-form educational content. Blog-style explanations about immigration and various news or press releases. All valuable content, but in this case, poorly placed.

Transactional visitors are ready to act.

They didn't need education. They needed direction.

We created a separate landing page, specifically for those ads, speaking directly to these visitors. We used a clear call to action—a big "Book Your Free Consultation Today" button next to bullet points about why it makes sense to do that—and the conversions jumped 32%. That was with the *same traffic, just better alignment with intent.*

Understanding visitor intent is crucial because it's exactly what search engines like Google are trying to do.

Google's guidelines introduce a 'Needs Met' scale to evaluate how well a search result satisfies the user's likely goal, whether it's informational, commercial, or transactional. Aligning your page content directly with that intent is key to providing a satisfying user experience. It's the very thing Google aims to measure and reward, but more importantly, what your users actually want.

Here's how to apply this approach to your own website:

1. Start by defining your primary visitor intent. What are most of your visitors likely thinking or doing when they first arrive? Are they learning, comparing, or ready to act?
2. Map your content and pages to these stages. If your visitors are mostly in the early stages, your site should offer educational content and helpful resources that build trust. If they're deeper in the funnel, you'll need focused landing pages with strong CTAs that move them to action.

3. If your audience spans all three intents, structure your site in a way that clearly guides each type of visitor to the content that suits them. Don't force everyone through the same funnel.
4. And finally, make sure each page has one clear purpose. If someone arrives with commercial or transactional intent, don't make them dig for a next step. *Make it obvious.* A clean layout, a clear headline, a strong CTA—these are what separate high-performing sites from the rest.

The better you understand your visitor's intent, the more effective your website will be.

So remember: a website without a clear purpose isn't just underperforming—it's failing silently.

Your job is to define that purpose, align your site around it, and use every page to move people forward.

In the next chapter, we'll zoom in on what your visitors are *really* thinking and how to design your entire site around that.

Chapter 2:
Thinking Like Your Visitors

Why Visitor-First Thinking Changes Everything

Most businesses build their websites from the inside out. They start with what they want to say. What they want to highlight. What they think looks impressive. But if there's one thing to remember, it's that everyone only cares about themselves.

Your visitors arrive on your site with their own goals, needs, expectations, and levels of urgency. If your site doesn't immediately align with those things, they're gone.

It's not personal. It's just how people use the web. We're impatient. We're busy. And we've learned to scan, not read.

That's why the real power of a high-performing website comes from shifting your perspective.

The moment you stop building your site around what *you* want and start building it around what *your visitors* need, everything changes.

The layout makes more sense. The copy becomes sharper. The navigation gets clearer. The calls to action write themselves.

The magic is in the empathy.

The funny part is that almost everybody reading this is now thinking that this was obvious. Nobody thinks they're making a website based on what *they* want.

But after building hundreds of websites, I can assure you—most of you are.

It's because everyone wants a flashy website.

And that's okay. Flashy websites can absolutely help you reach your goals. But you still have to focus on those goals.

And yes, this applies whether you're a solo freelancer or a multi-million-dollar brand.

In fact, the more stakeholders involved, the easier it is to drift and lose focus. Every department wants their stuff featured. Every manager wants a shoutout for their win. Before long, you're designing a site to satisfy the board, not the buyer.

Your visitors are on your website for one reason: to solve a problem or fulfill a need.

This is the absolute core of SQRG's philosophy. Raters are explicitly and repeatedly told to evaluate results from the *user's perspective*—to put themselves in the user's shoes and to focus entirely on *user needs and user intent*.

That's the mindset that will guide us through this chapter. From structure to strategy, and from layout to flow, we're going to look at your website through the eyes of the person it's actually for. *Your* user.

When you make that shift, things that felt vague or subjective—design decisions, messaging, content layout—suddenly become more clear.

You stop debating which version "looks better" and start asking, *Which version better helps our visitor take action?*

The good news is, you've already done a lot of the hard work.

If you followed the process from Chapter 1, you should now have a clear goal for your website—the one thing you most want it to do. You should also have a defined understanding of who your audience is, and what they're hoping to get from your site. And finally, you should recognize how their level of intent changes depending on when and how they find you.

Now it's time to use that insight to shape your website like a guided journey—not a brochure, not a menu of options, but a purposeful experience that anticipates your visitors' needs and helps them accomplish their goals (which, conveniently, align with yours).

In the next section, we'll look at how to use your visitors' intent to shape the structure of your site: what pages you need, how they're arranged, and how they move people toward action.

Mapping Intent to Structure

Once you understand who your visitor is and why they're coming to your website, the next step is figuring out how to guide them through it.

That starts with structure.

The pages you include, how they're organized, and how they connect to each other—all of it needs to reflect your visitor's intent. And not just their general intent, but the specific stage they're in when they land on your site.

Not everyone is arriving ready to buy. Some people are just starting their research. Others are comparing options. A few are already convinced. They just need the final nudge.

That's why every website should be built around a simple but powerful idea:

Structure your site based on the different stages of your visitor's journey.

To illustrate this, let's use a framework you're probably already familiar with, even if you haven't applied it to your website before: the funnel.

At the top of the funnel, you have visitors in the awareness stage. These people are problem-aware but not necessarily solution-aware. They might have found you through a blog post, a social media mention, or even a friend's recommendation. Their intent is informational. They're looking to learn. They're not ready for a sales pitch yet—but if you play your cards right, they will be.

The middle of the funnel is where comparison starts. These are your commercial-intent visitors. They know what kind of solution they need, and they're actively researching options. They're reading service pages, pricing breakdowns, and case studies. They're interested, but not sold.

At the bottom of the funnel are the transactional-intent visitors. These people already know what they want—they're just looking for the easiest path to action. A phone number. A "buy now" button. A demo booking form. If they can't find it quickly, they'll bounce.

Remember the Google 'Needs Met' ratings? The guidelines go into detail about how raters are supposed to assess whether a page fully satisfies the user's specific goal—be it informational ('Know'), action-oriented ('Do'), or navigational—and pages tailored to the user's intent are far more likely to be rated highly.

This is why your site architecture matters so much.

You can't treat every page like it's for every person. The homepage shouldn't be designed the same way as a blog post. A service overview shouldn't be crammed with the same content as an FAQ page.

Each part of your site should serve a clear purpose and a specific intent.

Let's take a real example. Say you're a marketing agency.

A visitor lands on a blog post titled *"How to Improve Your Website's Conversion Rate."* That person is likely in the awareness stage. They're not ready to hire anyone—they're still learning.

Your goal isn't to pitch them immediately. It's to provide real value, build trust, and guide them to the next logical step. Maybe that's reading another article. Maybe it's downloading a checklist. Maybe it's exploring your case studies.

Now compare that to someone who lands directly on your *Web Design Services* page. That person is probably in the commercial stage. They're comparing you to other agencies.

Here, you need to speak to credibility. You need clarity. You need proof. And you need to make it incredibly easy to take the next step if they're ready.

Or maybe someone searched for *"book a web design consult"* and clicked your ad. That's transactional intent. They don't want to scroll through ten paragraphs about your mission and vision. They just want to talk to someone. For that person, the CTA needs to be front and center—above the fold, obvious, and friction-free.

Now here's the key: all of these people can exist in the same website. But they need different pages. Different paths. Different experiences.

That's what mapping intent to structure is all about.

It's about designing a site that doesn't just look good, but one that *functions* like a journey. Each page has a role. Each click moves someone forward. And everything works together to support your one primary goal.

Think of your site like a museum. You don't walk into a museum and immediately see every artifact at once. There's a curated flow. Introductory exhibits. Deeper dives. Clear paths and signage to help you explore in whatever way makes sense for you.

A great website works the same way. It doesn't overwhelm—it guides.

Most websites fail not because they lack information, but because they throw it all at the visitor at once.

They treat every page like it has to do everything, which means it ends up doing nothing very well. When you map your structure around your visitors' intent, you give them what they need, when they need it, and nothing they don't.

That's the goal.

Figure 2. Visitor Intent Funnel

This figure breaks down the three types of intent, showing how user goals, example queries, and typical website pages align at each stage. Use it to better match your content and structure to what visitors are actually looking for.

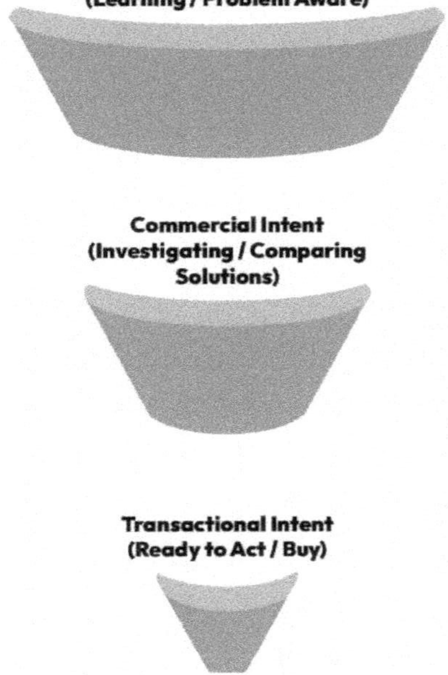

Informational Intent (Learning / Problem Aware)

User Goal:

Understand a topic, find answers, explore problems.

Example Queries:

"how to improve website conversion rate"
"what is user experience design"
"benefits of SEO for small business"
"learn about responsive web design"

Focus:

How, What, Why, Ideas, Tips, Benefits, Learn, exploring problems or general topics.

Typical Pages Suited For This Intent:

- Blog Posts
- In-depth Articles / Guides
- Resource Hubs / Libraries
- White Papers / Ebooks
- Glossary Pages
- Some FAQ Sections

Commercial Intent (Investigating / Comparing Solutions)

User Goal:

Evaluate options, compare features/providers, look for the best fit before making a decision.

Example Queries:

"best web design agencies for small business"
"Mailchimp vs ConvertKit comparison"
"top Shopify themes for cosmetics"
"HubSpot alternatives for startups"

Focus:

Best, Top, Vs, Comparison, Review, specific types of services/products, alternatives, pricing.

Typical Pages Suited For This Intent:

- Service Detail Pages
- Product Feature Pages
- Product Category / Collection Pages
- Comparison Guides
- Case Studies / Portfolio Pages
- Pricing Pages
- Testimonial / Customer Reviews Pages

Transactional Intent (Ready to Act / Buy)

User Goal:

Complete a specific action – purchase, sign up, contact, book.

Example Queries:

"hire UX consultant Los Angeles"
"buy [Specific Shoe Model Name]"
"sign up for Asana free trial"
"[Your Brand Name] discount code"
"emergency roof repair near me"

Focus:

Action verbs (Buy, Hire, Sign up, Download, Quote, Schedule), specific brand/product names, Discount, Coupon, Near me, Price.

Typical Pages Suited For This Intent:

- Product Pages
- Shopping Cart & Checkout Flow Pages
- Contact Us / Quote Request Forms
- Demo Booking / Consultation Scheduler Pages
- Free Trial Signup Pages
- Specific Landing Pages

Building a Guided Experience

Once your site is structured to support different levels of visitor intent, the next step is to make sure people can actually move through that structure.

That's where guided navigation comes in.

The biggest misconception about website navigation is that it only happens through the menu at the top of the page.

In reality, your visitors navigate your site through everything—calls to action, buttons, links inside your copy, visuals, even scroll cues. Every page on your site should intentionally guide people to the next logical step. If it doesn't, they'll either get lost or leave.

Think about it this way: when someone clicks through to your site, they're looking for something. Your job is to remove any obstacle that stands between them and that thing.

The best sites feel like they're *anticipating* what you're about to do, not waiting for you to guess where to go next.

That's why your homepage should act more like a train station than a billboard.

It shouldn't try to do everything at once. It should direct people, based on who they are and what they need, to the right part of your site. This could be a service page, a product, a case study, or even an educational article. What matters is that it's the right step for *them*.

Here's where most sites go wrong: they assume people will just figure it out.

They stuff all the important links into the main menu and leave it at that. But when you force users to rely on the navigation bar to find what they need, it usually means something's broken on the page they're on. The content didn't give them a clear next step. The CTA wasn't compelling, or worse, it didn't exist.

A better approach is to build pages that guide.

That means placing strategic links and buttons exactly where your visitor is likely to need them.

Think about what they're feeling at that moment. What questions might they have? What decision are they considering? The best link is the one that answers the question they haven't even asked yet.

For example, let's say you have a service page that describes how you help businesses improve their conversion rates. Halfway down the page, you show a short case study with a client who doubled their revenue. Right after that case study, there should be a call to action—something like, *"Want to see what we can do for your store?"* with a button to book a free consultation.

That's a guided experience. You gave them context, built trust, and then made the next step obvious.

This same thinking applies to blog posts, but you want to be careful about not blurring the lines here. They're just reading. They're likely just becoming aware, and hitting them with a CTA too soon may work in reverse.

If a visitor is reading an article about *"How to Speed Up Your Website,"* they're showing informational intent. But that doesn't mean they aren't also open to a solution. That article should focus on giving the answer and offering free value so that you address the intent of the visitor successfully, but it can absolutely also link to a related service page. Not at the top, where it feels like a hard sell, but maybe at the very bottom or even the sidebar.

Sometimes visitors will do the heavy lifting for you, and you can look for guidance in your analytics.

If you notice that a large percentage of visitors go from one page to another, even if those pages aren't currently linked, you should absolutely connect them. Add that link. Make it easier.

One of the simplest improvements you can make to any website is to reduce the time or the number of clicks it takes to get somewhere important. The less effort, the better the result.

This is what it means to build with intent. You're not leaving anything to chance. You're thinking through the path someone should take, and you're placing signposts along the way—quietly, consistently, confidently.

The best part? When you do this right, it doesn't just improve conversions. It improves trust. It creates a smoother, more intuitive experience that makes visitors feel like your site *just works*. That feeling is rare, and it's powerful.

Your messaging, copy, and layout all come together to support this journey, and to make sure nothing on the page is standing in the visitor's way.

Aligning Messaging With the Journey

There's one thing visitors hate more than confusion: wasted time.

And nothing wastes time quite like messaging that's out of sync with where they are in their journey.

Too often, websites serve the same message to every visitor, regardless of intent or awareness.

Someone just starting their research gets hit with an aggressive pitch. Someone ready to buy gets buried in fluff. Someone looking for social proof is asked to "get started" before they've even seen what you offer.

This isn't just a missed opportunity. It's friction.

And friction kills conversions.

If your website is structured around your primary goal and your audience's intent, your messaging should be doing the same. Every word on the page should be pulling in the same direction, nudging the visitor just one step closer to action—without pushing too far, too fast.

It starts with understanding where your visitor is in their decision-making process. Not just what they're looking for, but what they need to hear at that moment in order to feel good about taking the next step.

Let's say someone is just becoming aware of a problem. They're in research mode. They're not ready to buy, or talk to a salesperson.

What they need is clarity. They need to understand the problem better and see that you understand it, too.

This is where top-of-funnel content comes in. Guides, insights, comparison breakdowns, light storytelling—things that meet the visitor where they are. Your message at this point is, "We understand what you're facing. Here's what you need to know."

Further down the funnel, the dynamic shifts. Visitors are no longer exploring, they're evaluating. They've already compared a few options. This is where trust and confidence matter most.

For service businesses, that might mean case studies, testimonials, or process breakdowns that show what it's like to work with you. For product-based brands, that could mean customer reviews, user-generated photos, and clear return policies that remove hesitation.

Less education, more validation. Case studies. Testimonials. Specific results. Clear differentiators. Pricing clarity, process explanations. Your message now becomes, "Here's why we're the best choice, and what happens next."

And for visitors who are ready to act? That's when your messaging needs to get out of the way.

No storytelling. No scrolling marathons. Just clear headlines, crisp benefits, strong visuals, and an obvious next step. Add to cart. Book a demo. Start your trial. Whatever the action is, don't bury it in the background. Give them a path that feels easy.

But—and this is important—messaging isn't just about words. It's also about hierarchy, layout, and sequencing.

The best messaging doesn't need to shout because the structure already makes the journey feel natural.

For example, imagine a landing page where each scroll section builds trust. It starts with a simple statement of value. Then it reinforces that statement with a quick visual, then adds a bit of proof, and finally presents a single action step. You don't need to write a novel to convince someone—they convinced themselves as they moved down the page. The copy just supported the process.

It's also true here that at times an image is worth a thousand words. Especially true in eCommerce. It's a much stronger argument to show people using your products and solving their problems than it is for you to just claim that they do.

Messaging also needs to be consistent across pages. If your homepage promises one thing, but your service or product page feels like a different company wrote it, you're eroding trust.

Voice, tone, clarity—all of it needs to match. Think of your site as a conversation. You don't start friendly and focused, then switch to corporate and robotic halfway through.

You stay consistent. Reassuring. Human.

A great website doesn't just inform or persuade—it reassures. It says, "You're in the right place. Keep going." That's what good messaging does when it's aligned with the journey.

With that said, even with a solid structure and smart messaging, you're still making informed guesses. That's the nature of building a user-focused website. You'll never get everything right the first time, and that's okay.

The key is to start with intent.

Make decisions based on who your visitors are, what they want, and how they move through your site.

Then watch what happens.

Over time, the data will show you what needs to be improved. But for now, if you've done the work to structure your site with empathy, and you've crafted messaging that feels aligned to your users' journey, then you're in a better position than most.

In the next chapter, we'll take all this insight and look at how to structure your website in a way that makes everything feel intuitive, for both your visitors and your business.

Chapter 3:
Structuring Your Website

Building the Foundation - Pages That Matter

If your website is going to perform, it has to be made of the right parts. That starts with defining the actual pages your site needs—and cutting the ones it doesn't.

This is where we move from thinking about your website to actually shaping it.

At this stage, most businesses make one of two mistakes. Either they don't plan their pages at all and go with a generic layout, or they create too many pages (one for every idea or internal initiative, whether it's relevant to visitors or not).

The right approach is intentional.

Every page should serve one of these roles:

1. **Inform**: Answer questions and offer clarity
2. **Persuade**: Build trust and desire
3. **Convert**: Make the action easy and obvious

If a page doesn't clearly do one of those things, it likely doesn't need to exist.

Informational pages help answer questions and offer clarity. This could be a blog post, a help article, a product comparison, or even an FAQ. These types of pages support early-stage visitors and help bring in traffic through search.

Persuasive pages exist to build trust and generate desire. Think of core service pages, product pages, testimonials, or case studies. These are the pages that shape perception and move people toward considering action.

Conversion-focused pages are where business happens. This could be your checkout or your contact form.

Every page needs to earn its place.

Just because your competitor has a certain page doesn't mean you need it. Just because it existed on your last site doesn't mean it belongs on this one.

Now let's talk about how to decide what pages you actually need.

Start by going back to your website's primary goal. If your goal is to drive leads for a service-based business, then your site should focus on making it easy to understand what you offer, why you're credible, and how to take the next step.

I've seen this play out firsthand, where sometimes trimming a long page down to one screen can triple conversions. It's not about removing information; it's about removing distraction.

If you're an eCommerce brand, your site should be optimized around browsing, clear value proposition and proof, and seamless checkout—making sure nothing stands in the way of a transaction.

Let's say you're a boutique law firm with a strong focus on generating qualified leads. In that case, you'd structure your website to make it as easy as possible for someone to understand what you do, why they should trust you, and how to get in touch.

That might include separate pages that explain each of your services clearly, along with client testimonials, team credentials, or case studies that build authority. But those decisions should come from your specific strategy, not from a template or guesswork.

If your focus is on attracting top-tier corporate clients, the structure and content will look very different than if you're targeting individuals seeking help with personal injury claims.

The difference isn't just aesthetic—it's foundational. One audience may want detailed white papers and legal insights. The other may just need to feel confident they're in the right hands and know how to reach you quickly.

The same principle applies to eCommerce.

A store selling high-end skincare might need a more educational, brand-driven experience that builds trust and explains ingredients. A fast-fashion store? That's all about speed, clarity, and making it easy to browse and buy.

There's no one-size-fits-all approach, even though Shopify theme developers would love to convince you otherwise.

Your job is to define what your visitors need in order to say *yes*. And then structure your website around those steps—no more, no less.

And yet the core principle is the same: clarity.

Every page should either inform, persuade, or convert. If it's not doing one of those things, it's probably not worth keeping.

This doesn't mean you have to launch with a barebones site. You can, and should, include supporting content that enhances the experience.

For a service business, this might mean a few carefully written blog posts that cover your areas of expertise or address related issues that your prospects may have. For an online store, it might mean a quiz to help users find the right product, a comparison chart to differentiate your best sellers, or a blog post showing the latest and greatest products in your industry where the spotlight is on—you guessed it—your products.

These kinds of pages can be incredibly valuable, but only when they're tied back to your goal.

A blog post that gets traffic but leads nowhere is a missed opportunity. A gift guide that doesn't link directly to the products it features is a dead end.

Every page you include should play a defined role in the visitor's journey. If it's not helping the visitor move forward or deepening their trust, it's noise.

And the more noise you have, the harder it becomes for your visitor to hear what matters.

The great thing about it is that it also works in reverse.

If every page you have is helping the visitor move forward then they're likely to stay around longer. If they stay around longer then they're more likely to convert and help you achieve your goal. But it goes further—all of these things will also help you rank better on Google.

The reason is that if you write a great article that clearly addresses a problem and describes the solution then people will share it and Google will reward you for it. Same goes for that gift guide—people eat these up—and Google is all about giving people what they want.

If you manage to align what people are looking for with your products or services then you have a clear win-win-win, because you're making your website better, your visitors are more likely to buy, and Google is more likely to rank you higher and send you more free organic traffic.

Once again this is all aligned with Google's rater guidelines. They talk about the importance of Main Content quality and quantity; and they specifically call out pages lacking a clear purpose or containing "thin or unhelpful content" which are said to contribute negatively to the site's overall quality assessment. You want to make sure that all your pages earn their place and help signal a higher-quality, more user-focused site.

So before you wireframe anything, map out the pages that actually support your goal. Identify which ones are essential, which ones support the journey, and which ones can be cut entirely.

Be ruthless here—your website will be better for it.

Figure 3. Mapping and Addressing Common Objections

Use the table below as a model. I've filled in a few examples to show how it works. Now create your own version based on the specific doubts, hesitations, and needs of your audience.

Common Objection What's stopping them from taking the next step? What are they unsure about or afraid of?	**Priority Score** How damaging is this doubt? Is it a deal-breaker or just a mild hesitation? Rate it 0 to 5.	**Key Pages** Where do you plan to address this within the website?	**How to Address** Specifically how do you plan to address this within the website?
"Is this too expensive / Can I afford it?"	5	Pricing Page, Service Page	Clear value prop, Tier comparison, Financing options, ROI examples
"Can I trust this company is legitimate/ capable?"	5	About Page, Homepage, Service Page	Team bios, Client logos, Specific case studies, Testimonials
"What if I buy and don't like it?"	4	Product Page, FAQ, Checkout	Clear Return Policy link, Satisfaction Guarantee badge/text
"Will this actually work for someone like me?"	5	Homepage, Service/Product Pages, Case Studies	Showcase relatable customer stories, feature industry-specific case studies, use inclusive language ("made for businesses like yours").
"Is it complicated or time-consuming to get started?"	4	Onboarding Page, Homepage, Product Page	Explain the onboarding process clearly, use a "Getting Started is Easy" section, include quick-start videos or timelines.
"Am I locked into a long contract?"	3	Pricing Page, FAQ	Clearly state cancellation/refund terms, emphasize flexibility (month-to-month options if available), feature a "No Risk, No Commitment" message.
"Will I get support if I need help?	4	Contact Page, Product Page, Footer	Promote 24/7 support options, live chat, easy access to help center, introduce customer success team photos or bios.

Navigation, Hierarchy, and Priority

Once you've defined the pages your site actually needs, the next challenge is figuring out how to organize them, and how to help your visitors find them.

This is where navigation, page hierarchy, and visual priority come into play.

Done well, these elements guide your visitors effortlessly through your site. Done poorly, they lead to confusion, frustration, and lost opportunities.

The biggest mistake most businesses make is trying to cram everything into their navigation. They treat the menu bar like a table of contents, assuming more visibility equals better access. But more often than not, more links means more noise.

Your main navigation should only include your most important pages—the ones that either represent your primary goal or help support it directly.

If a visitor only sees your homepage and the links in your top menu, would they know what your business does and what to do next? If not, you've got some trimming to do.

Here's the rule: *the more important the page, the easier it should be to access.*

Think of your homepage and your navigation as your highest-priority real estate.

The top-level items in your menu are your main traffic lanes. Everything else should live underneath those or be accessible within one or two clicks, preferably in places that make contextual sense.

Let's say you run a SaaS platform that helps eCommerce businesses with inventory forecasting. You don't need "Privacy Policy," "Partners," "API Documentation," and

“Blog Categories” all listed in your main menu. You need links to your core product overview, pricing, a demo request page, and possibly a few trust-building resources like case studies or testimonials. Everything else can—and should—live in the footer or be found through guided content.

The same applies to eCommerce. If you sell hundreds of products, you need smart categories and subcategories, not a mega menu with every item listed. Your job is to help people start their shopping journey as smoothly as possible. That might mean breaking your store into clear sections—by collection, by use case, or even by gift type—depending on how your customers like to browse. But again, not every single collection needs a link in the main nav.

Hierarchy matters. Some pages deserve more prominence than others.

For example, your “About” page is helpful for trust and connection, but it’s rarely the thing that drives conversions. So maybe it doesn’t belong in the main navigation—it could live in the footer, or be linked contextually from a founder story or team section on the homepage.

On the other hand, a page that leads directly to your primary goal (like “Book a Demo” or “Start Shopping”) should be accessible from almost anywhere on the site, including the nav, hero sections, buttons, and even the sticky header on scroll.

This hierarchy also plays a role on your homepage. A lot of businesses try to say everything right on the homepage, thinking it’s their one shot to make an impression.

But the truth is that your homepage is a hub, not a destination. It should offer a clear value proposition and quickly guide people to the next step based on who they are and what they're looking for.

That means your homepage should prioritize clarity and pathways over depth.

Think of it like a well-designed airport terminal. No one's there to hang out. They're there to get somewhere.

Your job is to help them get to the right gate without confusion.

If your homepage tries to cram in full product descriptions, detailed service breakdowns, and five different CTAs, you're making people think too hard. Instead, give them enough to understand what you offer, and then guide them to the page that goes deeper.

You also want to consider multiple types of users. Not every visitor comes to your site with the same goal or level of knowledge.

Some might be returning customers who already know what they want. Others may be first-time visitors who need context before they commit to a next step. Your structure should make room for both, without overwhelming either.

For example, let's say you're an eCommerce site that sells outdoor gear. A returning customer might want a shortcut to reorder the same tent they bought last year. A new visitor might want to compare tents for a weekend camping trip. Your homepage might highlight new arrivals or bestselling products, while also offering a quick path to your collections page, and even featuring a quiz that helps first-timers figure out what gear is right for them.

For service businesses, this could mean showing a "Start Here" guide for new visitors while also giving returning users a "Book a Call" button right in the header.

The point is to guide different types of visitors without dumping everyone into the same one-size-fits-all funnel.

And remember—your navigation doesn't start and end with your top menu.

Your internal links, buttons, and page layout all play a role in guiding people forward. A visitor shouldn't need to go back to the menu to keep exploring. Ideally, every page on your site nudges them naturally toward the next best step.

This is why thoughtful hierarchy matters.

It gives your site structure. It helps people move smoothly. And it makes your website feel like it was designed for them, not just for your business.

Common Structural Issues (and How to Avoid Them)

Even when your pages are well-planned and your navigation is logically mapped out, it's still easy to fall into structural traps that degrade performance, overwhelm visitors, and kill momentum.

Let's look at some of the most common ones—and how to avoid them.

The first is the cluttered homepage.

This is everywhere. And it's easy to see why.

Everyone wants their piece of the spotlight. Marketing wants the promo banner. Sales wants the hero CTA. HR wants a link to careers. Support wants a help center button. Leadership wants a vision statement. And suddenly, the most important real estate on your site is jam-packed with internal politics and conflicting priorities.

But to the visitor, none of that matters. They don't care what every department wants. They care about finding what they came for.

A cluttered homepage is a symptom of unclear prioritization. It says, "We couldn't decide, so we included everything". And that's how you lose people.

The solution is ruthless clarity.

Strip your homepage down to the essentials. Focus it around the primary goal of the site. Show people what you do, why it matters, and what to do next, and let the rest of the site do the supporting work.

Another common issue is over-nesting.

This shows up in your site's hierarchy and navigation. It's when pages get buried multiple layers deep inside folders or dropdowns.

You might see a service page tucked under a category that's under another category. Or a product hidden three clicks away behind multiple filters. This isn't structure—it's a maze.

It might feel tidy from the back end. But to the visitor, it's friction.

And friction kills conversions.

Your most valuable pages should never be more than 2 clicks away from the homepage.

That doesn't mean you can't have depth, especially if you have a large product catalog or a detailed blog. But that depth should be accessible through guided navigation, internal links, and smart design—not just buried in the menu.

A perfect example is the collection navigation of an eCommerce store that has thousands of products of all types and kinds. Think of a Nordstrom, or Bloomingdales. Their navigation could span thousands of links, because they literally have tens of thousands of products, but if you actually pay attention you'll see that they all follow the same structure and that is sub-navigation within collections.

This is actually a very powerful SEO strategy too because, as we've seen with every other rule of SEO, it really helps the visitor.

Specifically, imagine how many types of dresses you may find at one of those department stores. Now go and take a look at any billion dollar store with thousands of products. They probably have a handful of key types of products in their navigation, and when you click through you'll see an additional navigation within the collection to drill down further. And then filters to narrow your focus too. For example, under Dresses, you may find a sub-navigation for formal dresses or casual dresses, and if you click through to those, you may have the option to narrow down further to floral casual dresses among many others.

These hyper-specific collection pages tend to rank fast on Google because of that very reason. Imagine someone searching for a leather long sleeve bridesmaid dress landing on a collection that specifically focuses on these dresses. It's the perfect result. And they are specifically looking for that, so they're very likely to buy.

Such guided navigation also helps address a common issue which is orphan pages.

An orphan page is a page that exists on your site but isn't linked to from anywhere meaningful.

It's live, but disconnected. No one can find it unless they know the exact URL or happen to land on it through search or an ad.

This is common with things like landing pages, old blog posts, press releases, or pages created for specific campaigns that were never retired or reintegrated.

It happens slowly, over time, especially in growing organizations. But over time, it clutters your site architecture, bloats your sitemap, and can even hurt your SEO.

Every page on your site should be connected to something.

If it's worth having, it's worth linking to. If it's not worth linking to, it's probably not worth keeping. It's ok to delete pages if they're no longer relevant.

Let's not forget about performance.

A bloated structure almost always leads to a bloated website. And that affects load time, crawlability, and overall user experience.

This is where the decisions you make about structure become deeply technical. If your site is filled with unnecessary pages, disorganized categories, outdated blog posts, and extra templates, then it's not just harder for visitors to navigate—it's harder for developers to maintain, for search engines to index, and for you to scale.

You're also more likely to end up with mismatched page designs, inconsistent CTAs, and clunky templates that feel more stitched together than streamlined.

All of this adds up to a kind of structural debt, the hidden cost of poor organization. And like technical debt, it grows over time.

The longer you wait to clean it up, the harder and more expensive it becomes.

This is why the structure of your website should be treated as a system, not a suggestion.

It's not just the layout of your nav or the shape of your sitemap—it's the connective tissue that holds everything together. If it's weak, everything else suffers.

Again, none of this means your site needs to be rigid or minimal. Great websites can have lots of content, lots of pages, and lots of complexity, as long as the structure supports it.

If your business has grown, your offerings have expanded, or your team wants more control, that's fine. But the structure should grow with intention. Every page, every section, and every link should exist because it helps someone get where they need to go.

That's the point of structure: not to limit creativity, but to channel it. To help your website perform at its best because it's focused, clear, and built for the people who use it.

When your site's foundation is solid, each page becomes easier to design, easier to optimize, and far more likely to convert.

In the next chapter, we'll zoom in from the big picture to the individual page, and look at how to guide attention, build trust, and drive action where it counts.

Chapter 4:
Crafting Pages That Drive Action

Introduction: Why Page Design Matters

Most websites are designed to look good. Fewer are designed to work. A high-performing website page isn't a static piece of art—it's a conversation. It anticipates what your visitor is thinking, responds with what they need to hear, and then gently nudges them toward taking action.

But none of that can happen unless you first understand how people actually interact with web pages.

Visitors don't read your pages, they scan them.

They don't navigate the site the way you planned. They click around based on curiosity, confusion, and whatever draws their attention first. They don't follow your "ideal journey" from top to bottom, left to right. They skim, jump around, and make decisions in seconds based on a gut feeling.

Understanding this behavior, and designing around it, is what separates pretty pages from profitable ones.

This matters because if you place something important (like your value proposition or your call to action) in a part of the page that the eye skips, you've essentially hidden the thing that matters most.

Designing pages that convert isn't about decorating the screen. It's about controlling attention.

This is where visual hierarchy comes in.

When everything on a page screams for attention, nothing gets it. A great page uses size, spacing, contrast, and positioning to guide the eye. The headline should be the biggest thing on the page. The next thing should be the subhead or a short explanation. The call to action should feel like a natural next step—not a hunt. A simple, logical layout makes the user feel like they're being guided. It creates confidence. It creates trust.

And trust is essential, because people don't make decisions logically, not at first. They react emotionally and then use logic to justify their decision.

That's why the top of the page, especially the hero section, is so critical. In the first few seconds, the page has to make people feel like they're in the right place. It has to give them a sense of clarity, connection, and direction.

When someone lands on your site, they're asking a few unspoken questions.

- Is this what I'm looking for?
- Can these people help me?
- Do I feel like I belong here?

If the design, the copy, or the layout gives even a whiff of friction, they're gone before they ever read your product description, your credentials, or your case studies.

That first moment is emotional. But if you get it right—if you make people feel seen—then they'll give you their attention. And once you have that, you can use logic to help them take the next step.

That's when it's time to show the features. That's when you talk about the benefits. That's when you explain how you're different and why you're worth it.

But none of that matters if the top of the page doesn't connect.

This applies whether you're selling a high-ticket consulting service or a ten-dollar t-shirt. The psychology is the same. Attention is limited. Decisions are emotional. Clarity wins.

So when we talk about crafting pages that drive action, we're not talking about where to put the button. We're talking about building an experience that makes people want to click it.

Crafting the Page Narrative That Converts

Every high-converting page tells a story.

Not in a flowery, once-upon-a-time kind of way, but in a structured, persuasive sequence that walks the visitor through a specific set of thoughts and emotions.

And while every website is different—different goals, different audiences, different offers—the structure of these stories is surprisingly consistent.

That's because people process information in similar ways. Whether someone is booking a software demo or buying a pair of sneakers, they still need to be oriented, convinced, and guided.

This consistency is most obvious at the top of the page—the first thing your visitor sees. Whether it's a homepage, a service page, or a product page, that top section has one job: to orient the visitor. To instantly signal what the page is about, who it's for, and what to do next.

Now, that doesn't mean it always looks the same. On a service page, orientation might come from a strong heading and a clear subheading. On an eCommerce product page, it might come from a striking photo or a short video. Sometimes the image is the headline.

You see this all the time on fashion or lifestyle product pages. The title and description are almost secondary. It's the image that does the heavy lifting: showing what the product is, how it fits, and why someone might want it.

The format changes, but the function doesn't.

That's the key. No matter the industry, the audience, or the device, every element at the top of the page plays the same role: to orient, to engage, and to move the visitor forward.

From there, the narrative unfolds and it's your job to guide it well.

When done right, that narrative follows a visual rhythm that aligns with how people naturally scan and read on the web.

Most visitors don't read word-for-word. Instead, they scan.

Their eyes track across the page in predictable patterns—patterns that research has shown repeatedly through eye-tracking studies.

The F-pattern is common on content-heavy pages like blog posts. Readers start at the top left, scan across the headline, then jump down the left edge, occasionally darting right to read something that catches their attention.

It's why clear headings and bolded keywords matter—they catch the eye along this pattern.

The Z-pattern, often seen on landing pages and sales pages, follows a different route. Visitors move from top left to top right, then diagonally across the page, and finally left to right again. This is especially common when a page has clear visual anchors in those zones—like logos, CTAs, and feature blocks. Understanding this movement helps you place key content, testimonials, and calls to action where they'll naturally be seen.

These scanning behaviors aren't just abstract theories—they directly shape how visitors process your content.

And if you align your structure with these natural movements, your content feels easier to consume. Your message lands faster. Your value becomes more obvious.

Aligning your page structure with these natural scanning behaviors helps users process information efficiently. It basically helps you achieve the page's purpose.

This ease of use and clear presentation are also positive signals considered within Google's Page Quality evaluations.

Remember: these "quality graders" have to quickly determine if the page satisfies their 'Needs Met'. They're also scanning, just like your actual visitors.

The key is to structure for scanning. Understanding how users scan and absorb content gives us a framework to follow. But of course there is more to it.

Even a well-scanned page can fall apart if it introduces doubt, confusion, or unnecessary work. That's where most websites lose momentum—and it's also where the biggest gains are hiding.

A beautifully structured page can still fail. And it usually fails quietly.

Not because it's broken, but because it introduces too much hesitation, too many decisions, or too little clarity.

Your page structure shouldn't be determined by design trends or guesswork. It should be shaped entirely by two things:

- What kind of page this is
- What your visitor is looking for at that particular moment

Let's start with product pages. If you're selling something straightforward, like a ceramic mug or a cotton t-shirt, then you don't need to overthink it. The product photo is doing most of the work. Maybe a few bullet points listing dimensions, material, shipping details, and price—that's it. The visitor isn't looking for a story. They just want to know, "Is this what I'm looking for? And how soon can I get it?"

But that all changes when the product gets more complex—or more expensive.

Say you're selling high-performance hiking boots. Now you're dealing with different types of customers: one cares about the waterproof membrane, another wants to know how it fits around the ankle, and someone else is comparing this boot to three others in a new tab.

In that case, you might follow the main image and product title with a breakdown of features, maybe some trust-building reviews, followed by a comparison chart or even a short demo video. You're not just showing a product. You're making a case for it.

This is where a lot of websites go wrong. They apply the same cookie-cutter structure to every product, every service, and every page—without considering the complexity of the offering or the mindset of the visitor.

The same principle applies to service-based businesses.

Let's say you're offering SEO services. The visitor lands on your service page, already intrigued. Maybe they clicked over from a blog post or an ad. What do they need to see right away? Probably some clarity on what the service includes, followed by proof that you've done it before. They need to feel like they're in the right place, and that reaching out isn't a waste of time.

But not every service requires the same trust-building steps.

If you're offering one-off consulting calls, for example, you don't need a five-section explainer with a full breakdown of methodology. A short paragraph on what they'll get, paired with a strong testimonial and an easy booking interface, may be enough.

It all depends on context.

That's why it's not just about the type of page—it's also about the *path* that led the visitor there.

If someone lands on a product page after reading a detailed feature breakdown in an earlier blog post, then they've already consumed a lot of information. In that case, keep it short. Reinforce the key points. Make it easy to buy.

On the other hand, if they're arriving cold, maybe from a search or an ad, then they might need more context before they're ready to act.

Same goes for services. If someone is coming from your homepage and clicking into your "Web Design Services" page, then chances are they're looking for a solution. That page needs to meet them with reassurance. A few lines on your process. A short list of deliverables. Maybe a client quote or two. All leading to one obvious next step: book a call.

You'll notice a pattern here: the page structure isn't fixed—it flexes depending on what the visitor knows, what they still need to know, and how confident they feel in taking the next step.

That next step might be buying a product. It might be scheduling a demo. It might just be learning a little more.

The point is, your job is to *guide* them, not overwhelm them, and definitely not leave them guessing.

The best pages are not the ones that "look best." They're the ones that help people move forward. Which means your structure, after the initial hook, should follow this general flow:

Reassure. Clarify. Guide.

Reassure them they're in the right place. Clarify what they're looking at and why it matters. Then guide them to whatever comes next.

What that looks like in practice will change from page to page. But the job is always the same: create a path, and make that path easy to follow.

Figure 4. The Reassure-Clarify-Guide Page Flow

Use this framework to analyze your key website pages. Does your page effectively move visitors through these three stages? Where might visitors get stuck or lack information? Ensure each page has clear elements addressing Reassurance, Clarification, and Guidance appropriate for its specific purpose and the visitor's likely intent.

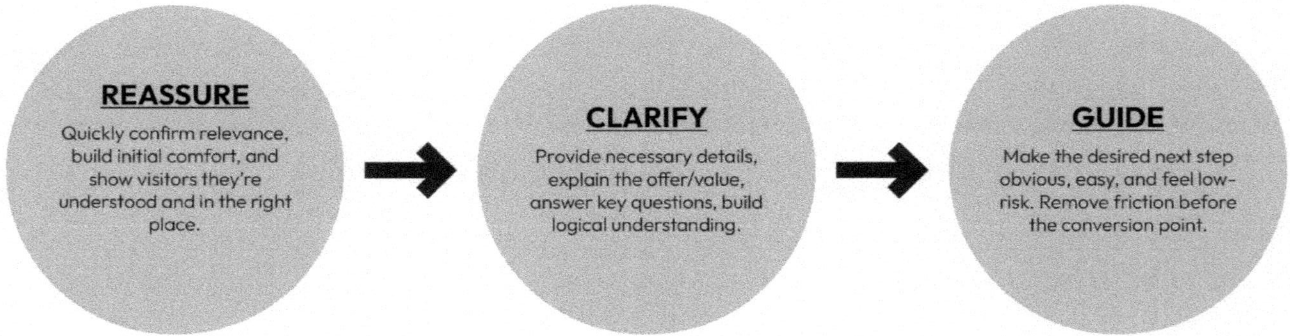

Key Visitor Questions Addressed:
"Is this what I expected/searched for?"
"Is this relevant to my problem/need?"
"Does this feel credible/professional at first glance?"

Typical Website Elements:
Strong, relevant Headline & Subheading
Compelling Hero Image/Visual
Clear opening Value Proposition
Clean, professional initial layout

Key Visitor Questions Addressed:
"What exactly is this product/service?"
How does it work / What are the key features?
"Why should I choose this over alternatives?"
"Is there proof it works?"

Typical Website Elements:
Benefit-focused descriptions
Clear feature lists/breakdowns
Concise explanation of process/methodology
Embedded testimonials or key stats
Well-structured, scannable text

Key Visitor Questions Addressed:
"What should I do now?"
"Is it easy to take the next step?"
"What happens when I click this button?"
"Is it safe / What's the commitment?"

Typical Website Elements:
Clear, Compelling Call-To-Action (CTA) Buttons
Benefit-oriented CTA copy
Text near CTA setting expectations
Trust seals or guarantees near conversion points

Micro-Decisions and the Invisible Obstacles That Kill Conversions

Sometimes a polished page can fail not because it's broken—but because it creates hesitation, overloads decisions, or lacks clarity. And when it fails, it often fails quietly.

When a visitor lands on a page, they're not asking "Do I trust this brand?" or "Is this the right service for me?" They're asking smaller, faster questions—ones they probably don't even realize they're asking.

- *Is this what I was expecting?*
- *Do I understand what this company is offering?*
- *Are they hiding the price because it's expensive?*
- *Does this feel safe?*
- *Is this going to waste my time?*

These are micro-decisions—dozens of them, layered into every scroll, every sentence, every pause.

And the websites that win are the ones that minimize the friction behind these moments.

One of the easiest ways to tank your conversions is to ask too much, too soon.

You see this all the time with service businesses: they have a huge "Book a Call" button front and center, but no real reason to click it. There's no context, no proof, no explanation of what happens next. For a visitor who just landed on the site, it feels like going from handshake to marriage proposal in 10 seconds.

It's the same problem with a lot of eCommerce product pages. The "Buy Now" button is in the right place, but everything around it feels vague or generic. There's no urgency, no storytelling, no reason to care. Even if the visitor *was* ready to buy, the lack of clarity is enough to stall them out.

Sometimes the CTA itself is the issue. "Submit", "Send", "Click here". These phrases don't feel like progress—they feel like risk. *What happens when I click? Am I going to be spammed? Is this a 10-step form? Do I need to talk to a salesperson?*

Ambiguity slows people down. The more questions they have, the more likely they are to bounce.

You also have to watch for what we call "dead zones." These are sections of a page where interest fades.

It's not that the content is bad. It's that the content is mistimed, misplaced, or misaligned.

Here's an example. Let's say your homepage opens strong. Clear promise, crisp value prop, solid CTA. But then, mid-scroll, you drop in a wall of dense copy—six long paragraphs of company history or market insight.

For most visitors, it's a brick wall. The flow stops. The energy dips. They scroll faster, looking for something more useful. Or they just leave.

Dead zones don't always look like content problems. Sometimes they're layout problems.

You bury an important feature behind tabs. You scatter key selling points across three columns. You make people hover to get basic info. These sound like minor UX issues, but they add up to friction.

And friction kills conversions.

And then there's the issue of trust signals that don't match the promise.

A service page might promise "world-class design," but the visuals look dated. A product might claim to be a bestseller, but there are no reviews. A brand might position itself as premium, but the copy reads like it was written in 2009.

Visitors notice these mismatches instantly, even if they can't articulate them. And once that trust dips, it rarely recovers.

The solution isn't to bombard your visitor with more stuff. It's to tighten the narrative.

Every element of the page should have a job. Every section should lead naturally to the next. Every decision, from heading to CTA, should feel like the obvious next step, not a gamble.

Ask yourself:

- *Are we asking for too much, too soon?*
- *Is every CTA aligned with the visitor's mindset at that moment?*
- *Are there any sections that slow the scroll or feel like a detour?*
- *Is anything on the page creating doubt or inconsistency?*

The best pages don't convince visitors to take action. They make action feel like the easiest, most natural thing to do.

And once you start spotting these micro-obstacles, you'll see them everywhere.

They're not dramatic. They don't scream. But they compound. And removing them is where the real magic happens.

These small points of friction don't just hurt conversion rates; they directly impact the user's ability to satisfy their needs efficiently and—you guessed it—they're a key factor in Google's 'Needs Met' assessment.

Friction can contribute to a confusing user experience which can lower the overall Page Quality rating and eat into the perceived Trustworthiness of the site - all signals that Google's guidelines take into account.

Want a good example that you've probably seen before? 100% money back guarantee no questions asked on the product page, with a fine print that suddenly appears on the checkout page.

And a very subtle example? Imagine a product page that emphasizes how "perfect" the item is for gifting, complete with language about special moments and presentation. But when you go to checkout, there's no gift wrapping option, no way to add a personal note, and no mention of how the product will be packaged.

Nothing there is technically wrong with it, but there's a quiet disconnect between the story you told and the experience you delivered. The result? A subtle erosion of trust. The buyer might not even be able to articulate why they hesitate—but they do.

Your focus should be to foresee that disconnect, before it happens.

Next, we'll zoom out again and look at how trust and momentum are built across the entire page, from top to bottom.

Because a good page doesn't just explain—it *pulls*.

The Psychology of Effective Page Design

High-converting pages aren't just well-written or well-designed—they're engineered.

And the best engineers of web experiences understand one thing above all: people behave in patterns.

When a visitor lands on your page, they're not reading it like a novel. They're scanning, darting around, following cues. They're making snap judgments based on how the page feels, whether it's clear or cluttered, trustworthy or off-putting, simple or confusing.

That's why strong pages don't just look good—they reduce cognitive load. They make it easier for the brain to process, evaluate, and act.

This is where visual hierarchy comes into play.

The size, weight, and placement of every element should guide attention. The headline should pull the eye. The supporting subheading should invite a nod of agreement. The next block—whether it's a testimonial, product image, or service overview—should feel like the obvious next stop on the journey.

If your visitor ever has to pause and ask, "What am I looking at?"—something's off.

It's not about manipulating behavior. It's about removing resistance.

You're not forcing visitors to convert, you're helping them reach the decision they already came here to make.

One more thing: great pages feel active. Not cluttered. Not loud. Just intentional. Every element should pull its weight. If something isn't helping the user make progress—through clarity, confidence, or momentum—it probably doesn't belong.

You've likely heard the phrase "don't make me think." That applies here, but not in a reductive way.

The goal isn't to dumb things down. The goal is to create a flow so intuitive that the visitor forgets they're even making decisions. They're just moving forward—step by step, click by click—because it all makes sense.

And that's the sweet spot: when your design, your copy, and your structure all work together and are no longer just a layout, but rather a guided experience.

In the next chapter, we'll shift from layout to language—and look at how great copy turns attention into results.

Chapter 5:
Writing Copy That Converts

Why Design Without Copy Is Half a Conversation

Design is what gets attention. But copy is what turns that attention into action. This is where so many websites fall flat.

They spend months refining the layout, agonizing over colors and spacing, and making sure everything "feels premium."

But then the copy, the actual words on the page, is slapped together at the last minute. It's vague. It's generic. It sounds like every other website in the category. And most importantly, it doesn't actually *say* anything.

A beautiful design might impress your visitor. But great copy makes them stay.

In fact, when we simplified our "free homepage" offer to just one headline, a single paragraph, and a 60-second video, the conversion rate jumped from 1% to 7%. The words didn't just describe the offer—they did the heavy lifting.

It's what tells them who you are, what you offer, why it matters, and what they should do next. It's the connective tissue between curiosity and conversion. Without it, your website is just a pretty picture with no substance.

And yet, most businesses treat copy like filler. Something you figure out *after* the design is done.

This is backwards. Because while design gets the user to look, it's the words that get them to move.

That doesn't mean copy has to come *before* design in every case, but it should never come last.

There's a healthy middle ground: rough out the copy first, even if it's just a draft. Let that guide the design. Once the layout is in place, refine the copy to fit it—but don't let visuals override the message. Otherwise, you end up with something beautiful that doesn't actually say anything meaningful.

Think about how people actually use websites. They scan the headline to get their bearings. They glance at a subheading to understand what's being offered. They read the short paragraph underneath to see if it's relevant.

If they're hooked, they'll keep scrolling. If not, they bounce.

The best copy doesn't try to be clever. It tries to be clear. Its job is to reduce doubt, increase desire, and remove friction, one sentence at a time.

And that can't happen if it's buried in design fluff or buzzwords that sound impressive but say nothing.

This focus on clarity isn't just about effective communication; it's a core component of Google's quality guidelines too. They emphasize that high-quality main content should be clear, accurate, and easily understood by the user. Vague or jargon-filled copy would fail this test, and could also undermine the site's perceived Trustworthiness.

Here's the truth: good copy doesn't sound like "copy".

It sounds like clarity. It sounds like someone saying exactly what you were hoping to hear, in the moment you needed to hear it.

This is especially important in today's digital landscape. People don't *read* websites. They scan. They skim. They're looking for cues—little moments of recognition that say, "Yes, this is for me."

And those cues almost always come from the words, not the visuals.

That's why the copy should never be an afterthought. It should shape the design, not chase it.

In the chapters before this, we talked about structure, goals, and the user journey. Those things don't come to life through layout alone. They come to life when you speak to your visitors in a way that's clear, confident, and grounded in their reality.

You can't Photoshop trust. You have to say something that earns it.

So before you obsess over the shade of blue or the width of a button, step back and ask:

What does this page need to communicate? What does my visitor need to hear in order to move forward?

Because when the words are strong, everything else becomes easier. The design falls into place. The navigation makes sense. The user keeps scrolling. And most importantly, they convert.

Great websites aren't just designed—they're written.

Writing For Clarity, Not Cleverness

There's a dangerous misconception in marketing that clever copy is effective copy. That puns, wordplay, and "brand personality" are what hook people.

But the truth is, when someone visits your website, they're not looking to be impressed. They're looking to be understood.

The most effective copy doesn't try to sound smart—it tries to make the reader feel smart.

It speaks in plain language. It answers questions before they're asked. It removes uncertainty instead of adding flair.

Because on the web, clarity is what builds confidence. And confidence is what leads to action.

One of the biggest red flags in copywriting is when a sentence makes you pause and go, "Wait, what does that mean?"

It happens all the time.

Agencies say things like "We empower digital transformation at scale." What does that actually mean? Nothing. It's copy for the sake of copy. It sounds expensive but says nothing useful.

Now compare that to something like: "We help B2B companies turn more website visitors into leads."

There's no poetry there. But it's specific. It's grounded. And more importantly, it tells the visitor exactly what the company does and who it's for.

This doesn't mean your copy has to be boring. But it does mean that clarity comes first. Your tone, your personality, your humor—those are layers. Not foundations. They only work if the core message underneath is solid and easy to grasp.

You also want to make sure your copy speaks **to** the visitor, not just **about** you.

A surprising number of websites still write from the inside out. "We've been in business for 20 years." "We're passionate about innovation." That might sound nice, but it's not useful unless it connects to what the visitor actually cares about.

The fix is simple: shift the lens.

Instead of asking, "What do we want to say?" ask, "What does the visitor need to hear in order to move forward?" That's how you go from talking **at** your audience to speaking **with** them.

Let's say you're selling a skincare product. Instead of writing, "Our serum uses cutting-edge biotech formulation with advanced hydration complexes," you could say, "Fewer breakouts. Smoother skin. Visible results in two weeks."

One version talks about the product. The other talks about the result. Guess which one converts better?

When in doubt, read your copy out loud.

If it sounds like something a real person would say to another real person, you're probably on the right track. If it sounds like a press release or a pitch deck, try again.

Because at the end of the day, your website isn't a presentation. It's a conversation.

And the best conversations don't confuse you. They connect with you. They feel like someone understands what you want—and can actually help you get it.

That's what good copy does. It doesn't try to be clever. It just makes sense.

And that's what makes it powerful.

Writing for Real People, Not Personas

A lot of businesses write their website copy for an imaginary persona pulled from a strategy deck. They try to sound strategic, polished, on-brand.

But in doing so, they lose touch with how real people actually talk—and what they actually care about.

The most persuasive copy doesn't sound like it came from a brainstorming session. It sounds like something you'd say out loud, in a real conversation, with someone who actually needs what you offer.

That's why the smartest marketers don't just rely on buyer personas or competitor websites for inspiration.

They talk to their customers. They read support tickets. They dig through reviews and testimonials.

Because buried in those conversations is the language people actually use to describe their problems, their goals, and the reasons they buy.

This is called voice of customer data—and it's pure gold.

When you reflect someone's exact language back to them, it creates an instant sense of understanding. It shows that you get it. And that's often what builds trust faster than any fancy headline or visual ever could.

Writing in the language your audience actually uses does more than just resonate; it signals expertise and builds credibility.

Google's guidelines emphasize E-E-A-T (Experience, Expertise, Authoritativeness, Trustworthiness), and demonstrating a deep understanding of user needs. It shows you 'get it,' which is fundamental to building trust online.

But to do that, you have to stop writing like a marketer and start writing like a human.

That means cutting the fluff. Skipping the buzzwords. Saying things simply, without dumbing them down. And most importantly, resisting the urge to impress.

One of the biggest copy traps is what's known as the *curse of knowledge*. That's when you're so familiar with your offer, or your industry, that you forget what it's like to be on the outside. So you write in technical language. You use acronyms. You describe features without explaining what they actually mean.

And when that happens, your copy loses people—not because they aren't interested, but because they don't understand you.

The fix is simple: say what you mean.

If your product helps people save time, say that. If your service helps businesses grow faster, say that. You don't need to dress it up in abstract language. You just need to speak to the outcome your audience already wants, and show how you help them get there.

You can still be creative. You can still have personality. But clarity has to come first. Always.

Because in the end, the most effective copy doesn't just sound good. It *feels right*—like you're speaking directly to the person reading it, saying exactly what they needed to hear, right when they needed to hear it.

Page-by-Page Copy Strategy

Not every page on your site needs to sound the same, but every page should follow the same rule: say the right thing, at the right time, to the right person.

Let's start with the homepage. This is often the most misunderstood (and overdesigned) page on any website. It's not a full sales pitch. It's not an art gallery. If you were to ask my clients they'll tell you that I often call it a map.

Your homepage needs to establish who you are, what you do, and who you do it for—fast.

If a visitor can't figure that out in five seconds, you've already lost them. You don't need to say everything. You just need to make it clear enough so they know where to go next.

Great homepages don't convert on their own. They guide people to the page that will.

On product pages, clarity becomes even more critical. But what most brands get wrong is focusing too much on features.

You don't need to tell people your mug is ceramic—they can see that in the photo. What you do need to say is why it's better than the five other mugs they're also looking at. Is it made from a specific kind of clay? Does it keep coffee hotter longer? Was it designed by someone they've heard of?

Your job is to turn features into benefits—and benefits into reasons to buy.

If someone has a question or concern about the product, your copy should answer it before they even have to ask. Reviews and trust badges help, but it's the copy that connects the dots.

Service pages have their own challenges. People aren't just buying a thing—they're buying you. That means your copy needs to do more than describe what you do. It needs to establish credibility, build trust, and reduce risk.

Visitors should leave the page feeling confident in your ability and clear about what happens next. A strong intro that clarifies the outcome, a breakdown of how the service works, maybe a testimonial or a relevant case study—these are the building blocks. And just like with product pages, your job is to anticipate the questions and remove the doubt.

Then there's the about page. This is the page where most brands make it all about themselves, and that's a mistake.

Your about page isn't about you. It's about why you're the right fit for them. That means your copy should still be visitor-focused. Tell your story, sure, but frame it around the values, experience, or approach that matters to your audience. They don't need your life story. They need a reason to believe.

And finally, we get to the calls to action. The copy here matters more than you think.

"Submit" is not a call to action. Neither is "Click here."

The best CTAs make the next step feel easy, safe, and valuable. Tell the user what happens next. Set expectations. Reduce the perceived risk. Instead of "Schedule a Call," try "See if we're a good fit". Instead of "Buy Now," try "Get Yours in 2 Days". The words you use can shift the entire feeling of the ask.

Tailoring your copy to your visitor's most likely intent is critical - clear, benefit-driven copy and unambiguous calls to action help users achieve their goals efficiently, and signal a high-quality, helpful page. It gets you bonus points for your "Needs Met" evaluation from Google too.

The structure of your site creates the path. The design helps people walk it. But it's the copy that gives them a reason to take the next step.

And when you treat each page like its own focused conversation, your site becomes something far more persuasive than any template—it becomes personal.

The Most Common Copy Mistakes I've Seen

The fastest way to ruin a strong design is to fill it with weak copy.

And weak copy doesn't always look bad—it just doesn't work.

The most common mistake? Trying to be clever instead of clear. You've seen it before: websites with vague headlines like "Reimagining What's Possible" or "Built for the Future."

These phrases might sound good in a pitch deck, but they mean nothing to a new visitor. If your copy doesn't tell them what you actually do, they'll leave.

You don't need to impress them—you need to inform them.

Then there's jargon. The industry speak. The buzzwords. The terms that make sense to you and your team but mean nothing to your audience. If someone has to stop and decode what you're saying, you've already lost them.

Clear beats clever. Plain beats polished. Every time.

Another trap is what we call "bloated intros." This is where pages open with long-winded paragraphs that say very little. They usually start with a version of "We understand how hard it is..." or "In today's fast-paced digital world..." These openers try to create empathy, but they're too generic to connect.

Visitors don't want a buildup. They want answers. Fast.

Passive language is another killer. Phrases like "solutions are offered" or "services are provided" feel distant and unsure. Strong copy uses active language. Not "Our platform is designed to streamline..."—just say what it does.

Be direct. Be confident. Take ownership of the message.

A lot of sites also suffer from what we call "explain paralysis." They over-explain everything. They assume the visitor needs a full essay before they can decide.

So they pile on paragraph after paragraph, hoping the volume of information will do the selling. But more words don't create more clarity. Often, they just create more friction. If your copy doesn't move the visitor forward, it's just in the way.

On the flip side, some sites say almost nothing. They try to be minimalist, but they end up being vague. No real offer. No clear CTA. Just pretty visuals and a few vague lines about "creating impact" or "driving innovation."

That's not branding—it's a missed opportunity.

The smallest edits can make the biggest difference. Changing "Learn More" to "See How It Works" tells the user what they're getting. Shifting from "Contact Us" to "Get a Free Quote" sets expectations and adds value.

These aren't just cosmetic tweaks, they're conversion upgrades.

In fact, just changing a button from 'Learn More' to 'See How It Works' increased click-through rates by 17% for one of our SaaS clients.

That's a 30-second fix with a double-digit return.

Ultimately, your copy should do one thing: move the visitor forward.

Anything that doesn't do that—any phrase, section, or sentence—needs to be questioned. If it's not helping, it's hurting.

Because great websites aren't just filled with content. They're stripped of everything that gets in the way.

Making It Scannable, Not Skimmable

People don't read websites. They scan them.

You've heard that before in this book, and that's on purpose. It's a truth worth repeating.

That's not a flaw in your audience. It's a feature of how we all consume content online.

We're busy. We're impatient. We don't want to work to figure out what a page is trying to say. That's why the best websites aren't just well-written—they're well-structured.

Scannable copy doesn't mean less copy. It means copy that's easy to absorb.

Think of your layout as a rhythm. Headline. Short paragraph. Subheading. Maybe a sentence in italics for contrast. Then another short paragraph.

The best sites create a reading cadence that feels effortless. Your visitor doesn't have to try, they just keep moving forward.

That movement is the key. Because when someone pauses, it's usually because of confusion or fatigue. If the layout is dense, the paragraphs are long, and the copy feels like a wall of text, they'll either skim without understanding or stop altogether.

Instead, your job is to create momentum.

That means short paragraphs, clear visual breaks, and thoughtful pacing. It means using subheadings to reset attention, and varying your sentence lengths so the rhythm doesn't go flat. It also means making room for "micro CTAs"—little nudges that reinforce progress and guide the next step. These might be a subtle link midparagraph, a testimonial near a value prop, or even a short one-liner that tees up the next section.

Structuring your copy for scannability directly impacts its perceived quality and usability.

In fact, Google's guidelines consider the overall organization and presentation of your "Main Content"; they are looking for copy that is easy to scan and digest because this allows users to find information efficiently, and ultimately contributes to a higher Page Quality assessment.

This matters just as much for eCommerce as it does for service businesses. A product description should be broken into digestible pieces—not shoved into one block of text. If you're selling something complex, help people find the detail they care about fast. If it's simple, make it easy to glance and buy.

The same applies to service pages. You're not writing a pitch deck. You're building trust in stages. Let each section do one job. Don't cram ten points into one paragraph—spread them out. Use the layout to let the message breathe.

Because when it's easy to scan, it's easier to believe.

And when it's easier to believe, it's easier to convert.

Then again, belief takes more than clarity. It takes trust. The kind of trust that's felt in every detail of your site.

That's what we'll explore next: how to build real, lasting credibility across every page.

Voice of Customer (VoC) Mining & Copywriting Exercise

Your customers are telling you exactly how to sell to them - you just need to listen! Using their exact language builds instant trust and shows you 'get it'. This exercise shows you how to mine customer feedback for pain points and desired outcomes, and then use that language to write compelling copy.

Where can you find your customers' actual words?

- Online Reviews (e.g., Google, Yelp, Amazon, G2, Capterra)
- Testimonials / Case Studies
- Social Media
- Forum Posts (e.g., Reddit, Quora)
- Customer Support Tickets / Chats
- Sales Call Recordings / Notes
- Customer Surveys / Feedback Forms

Let's look at made-up reviews for a fictional product: 'The SleepWell Smart Pillow'. Notice how we **bold pain points** (problems the customer had *before* or issues solved) and <u>underline desired outcomes/benefits</u> (what the customer gained).

Review 1:

"I used to **toss and turn all night**, waking up with a **sore neck**. Since using the SleepWell, I fall asleep faster and wake up feeling actually rested. Game changer!"

(Pain: Toss and Turn/Sore neck - Benefit: Wake up rested)

Review 2:

"My partner hated my **loud snoring**. It was **embarrassing**. The support in this pillow has made a huge difference – I'm much quieter now, and we both sleep better."

(Pain: Snoring - Benefit: Sleep better)

Review 3:

"This pillow is okay. Mostly bought it because I **kept having to replace** my cheap ones every few months. Hopefully this one actually lasts."

(Pain: Replacing pillows)

Review 4:

"Finally! A pillow that's actually comfortable and lets me sleep through the night without **turning every few minutes**. Best purchase I've made for my sleep in years."

(Pain: Constant turning - Benefit: Sleep through the night)

Review 5:

"This hits the spot! My old **memory foam pillow would get so hot** during the summer months, but no issues here."

(Pain: Hot pillow - Benefit: Stays cool [implied])

Review 6:

"It's definitely firmer than I expected, which took a night to get used to, but wow, the support is amazing for my **neck issues**. Best sleep I've had in months."

(Pain: Neck issues; - Benefit: Best sleep)

Review 7:

"For years I assumed **waking up with neck pain** was just normal. I tried this pillow on a recommendation and the difference is incredible. I wake up feeling refreshed and almost completely pain-free."

(Pain: Neck pain; - Benefit: Wake up refreshed / Pain-free)

Let's break these down.

Recurring Pain Points: Sore neck / Neck issues / Neck pain (Reviews 1, 6, 7); Tossing and turning / Readjusting (Review 1, 4)

Recurring Benefits: Wake up rested / refreshed / pain-free (Reviews 1, 7); Sleep better / through the night (Reviews 1, 2, 4)

If you notice pain points or benefits that your customers voice regularly then they must be included in your headlines - your headlines are your first point of contact and your chance to make that first impression.

For our imaginary SleepWell Pillow, a good headline could be: Want To Finally Sleep Through the Night & Wake Up Pain-Free? Say Hello To SleepWell.

Then we could follow it up with our Body Copy, where we get to sprinkle in more pain points and benefits:

Are you tired of waking up with a sore neck after tossing and turning all night? Stop replacing cheap pillows that go flat or get miserably hot.

The SleepWell Smart Pillow provides amazing support specifically designed for neck issues, helping you sleep better, stay cool, and finally wake up feeling rested and pain-free.

Customers say it's a "game changer" for achieving comfortable, quiet sleep. Invest in rest that lasts.

Notice what we did here. This is broken into 3 parts - one that starts by addressing pain points, then proposes the solution and its benefits, and concludes with some social proof. All based on what our customers are saying, which makes it feel as if you're specifically speaking to them - you heard them, and this is the solution they've been looking for.

That's what good copy does. It speaks to the customer - acknowledges their issues - and presents them with the best solution for them.

Chapter 6:
Building Trust and Credibility

The Real Role of Trust

Trust is the foundation of every decision your visitor makes. It doesn't begin when a visitor sees your best testimonial. It begins the moment your site loads.

The page either feels real... or it doesn't.

That sounds obvious, but most websites treat trust like a box to check—slap on a testimonial, maybe a security badge, and call it a day. But real trust isn't built in one place. It's built, or lost, everywhere. In the first second of the visit. In the way the headline is phrased. In whether the page feels cohesive. In how the copy sounds. Even in how fast it loads (we'll dive into that in the next chapter).

This "holistic sense of credibility" is exactly what Google focuses on with its E-E-A-T framework (Experience, Expertise, Authoritativeness, and Trustworthiness), which is outlined in the Search Quality Rater Guidelines and made for a big buzz word all over the SEO community in the last couple of years. It's essentially a core lens through which page quality is assessed. While specific proof points matter, the overall Trustworthiness (T) signal comes from the sum of it all—the clarity, the professionalism, the user experience—making the visitor feel confident and secure.

When people land on your website, they're not consciously asking, *Can I trust this brand?* They're absorbing cues. They're scanning for red flags and green lights. Their gut is doing the work long before their brain catches up. And that gut is influenced by dozens of micro-signals: Does this look legit? Does this feel modern? Is this for someone like me? Do they seem to know what they're doing?

If the answer to any of those questions is "I'm not sure," the visitor backs away. Not because they've decided you're untrustworthy—but because you didn't give them a reason to stay.

Take this in for a moment, because it's very important.

Visitors don't come to your site with a checklist: "Do they have five reviews? Are there security badges? Is there a client quote near the CTA?" No one is doing that. Instead, they're scanning quickly, processing instinctively. They're asking a deeper question: Does this feel like someone I can trust?

Trust is emotional first, logical second. People decide based on feeling, then justify with facts. That's why a fast-loading, clean-looking site feels more trustworthy, even before the visitor has read a single word. It's not just what you say. It's how you say it, how it looks, how it flows.

And here's the part most businesses miss: trust isn't just about being impressive. Trying too hard is often the problem.

There's a kind of insecurity you can feel on a lot of websites. Every headline screams. Every badge is trying to convince you. Every sentence is built to persuade. It feels like the brand is trying to prove something, because deep down, they're afraid they haven't. That desperation shows. It undermines credibility, even if the content is technically correct.

The strongest brands don't scream for trust. They project it quietly, through clarity and calmness.

You'll notice it in the tone. Confident, but not boastful. Clear, but not simplistic. No fluff, no filler—just real language that makes the visitor feel like they're in good hands.

You'll see it in the layout. Nothing feels rushed or thrown together. Spacing is intentional. Elements have room to breathe. The design doesn't feel trendy for the sake of it. It feels like it belongs to the brand.

It's about being *clear*. Clarity is what builds confidence. When your content is straightforward (using clear copy, targeted visuals), your offer is easy to understand, and your path forward is obvious, the visitor feels safe. They're not bracing for a catch. They're not second-guessing your intentions. They know what they're getting into.

Trust also comes from seeing proof, but not just statements or testimonials. Oftentimes it's proof to back what you're saying, as you're saying it.

When a brand says they deliver world-class customer service, the visitor wants to see what that actually means. How fast are response times? What does support look like? Can I find a real story or quote that illustrates it?

Same goes for quality. If you say your product is "industry-leading," how can I know that? Is there a stat? A case study? A before-and-after result that shows impact?

People don't just want claims. They want clues. And those clues are often more subtle than marketers think.

A thoughtful headline can do more than a flashy video. A well-written paragraph can outperform an entire row of social proof. It all depends on whether it feels honest, direct, and grounded in reality.

And that's the key: trust isn't a widget. It's a signal. It's something you emit across every inch of your site. It's in the photo that doesn't look like a stock image. It's in the language that doesn't sound like marketing speak. It's in the smoothness of the scroll, the responsiveness of the interface, the effort it took to make the site feel frictionless.

It's even in the silence—what you *don't* say.

That's why the best trust-building websites show up with clarity, calmness, and confidence. They feel put together. Aligned. Real.

And when a site feels real, people are drawn in.

Because trust isn't a feature of your website. It's the byproduct of every choice you make.

The best trust-building websites don't feel like they're trying to sell you something. They feel like they're trying to help you make a good decision.

And that shift—from convincing to guiding—is everything.

So yes, testimonials matter. Social proof matters. Case studies and reviews and client logos matter. But they only work when the rest of the site already feels credible. They're not the foundation of trust. They're the reinforcement.

The foundation is emotional. It's what your visitor picks up in the first five seconds. Before they read your quote. Before they even reach your footer.

Does this feel real?

If the answer is yes, then everything else starts to work harder.

Demonstrating strong E-E-A-T builds credibility with both users and search engines. It's a key lens to assess website and content quality.

Figure 5. E-E-A-T Audit & Action Plan Worksheet

Use this worksheet to understand each component, see examples of how it applies online, evaluate your current site, and brainstorm ways to improve.

	Experience (E)	**Expertise (E)**	**Authoritativeness (A)**	**Trustworthiness (T)**
Definition	Demonstrating first-hand, real-world experience with the topic, product, or service. Showing you've actually "done the thing."	Demonstrating deep knowledge, skill, and credentials in the subject matter. Being an expert in the field.	Being recognized as a go-to source or leader in your field by others. Your site/brand's reputation.	Making users feel safe, secure, and confident in your website and the information/ service provided. Being honest and reliable.
Examples	• Detailed case studies showing process and hands-on involvement. • Author bios highlighting relevant practical background. • User-generated content (e.g., reviews with photos/ videos of product use). • "Behind-the-scenes" content showing product creation or service delivery. • Content written from a clear first-person perspective sharing personal learnings.	• In-depth, comprehensive articles, guides, or tutorials. • Displaying relevant credentials, certifications, or education. • Author bylines linked to detailed author pages/ bios. • Original research, data, or unique insights. • Accurate, well-cited information (especially for complex topics).	• Mentions or links from other well-respected websites in your industry (backlinks - see Ch 7). • Positive reviews and high ratings on reputable third-party sites. • Awards, recognitions, or accolades. • Being cited as a source by others. • Featuring testimonials from recognized industry figures (if applicable). • Clear information about the website owner/organization.	• Easy-to-find, clear contact information. • Secure connection (HTTPS). • Transparent Privacy Policy, Terms of Service, Return/ Refund Policy. • Professional, error-free website design and functionality. • Clear authorship for articles/content. • Positive customer reviews and testimonials. • Guarantees or warranties offered. • Secure checkout process with recognized payment options.

Clarity Over Bravado

Most businesses think that building credibility means sounding important.

So they stuff their copy with jargon. They pad it with buzzwords. They go out of their way to sound like a "market leader" or an "innovative disruptor."

And in doing so, they bury the very thing that would actually make people trust them: **clarity**.

People don't trust what they don't understand. When your language is vague, inflated, or overly technical, it makes visitors feel like outsiders. And when someone feels like an outsider, they're not leaning in—they're backing away.

Clarity is not just a writing principle. It's a trust principle.

Think of it this way: when you land on a website and immediately understand what the company does, who it's for, and why it matters—you relax. You feel oriented. You feel like this company knows who they are. You start to trust them. But if you land and have to re-read the first sentence three times just to figure out what industry they're in, the clock is already ticking—and it's counting down to a bounce.

This happens constantly with B2B service companies. They lead with their "platform for end-to-end lifecycle enablement" instead of saying, "We help SaaS companies onboard customers faster." One of those builds trust. The other builds confusion.

Now, this doesn't mean your copy has to be boring. Simplicity doesn't mean blandness. The goal isn't to strip your message down until it's dry and lifeless—it's to make sure it actually communicates something real.

There's a difference between being beautifully written and being beautifully vague. Great copy can absolutely be luxurious, elevated, even poetic.

A brand selling high-end candles doesn't need to sound like a tech spec sheet. It should evoke something—mood, feeling, ambiance. "A candle that smells like fresh basil and the ocean" is fine. "A candle that evokes sunlit gardens and open windows on a Sunday morning" might connect more deeply. The point is, both describe the same product, but one creates a moment. One gives you a reason to care.

The problem isn't fancy language. The problem is empty language.

Phrases like "delivering next-level innovation" or "revolutionizing tomorrow" don't actually say anything. They try to impress instead of inform. And when you rely too much on that kind of copy, your visitor might not be confused—but they won't be convinced either. They'll nod politely, then click away.

If you want to sound premium, sound premium. If your tone is playful, go playful. But ground it in substance. If you're promising a feeling, show what creates it. If your product is life-changing, say how. If your service is award-winning, say why. People will appreciate your creativity, but only if there's clarity underneath it.

That's why your first job in building credibility is to remove friction from your message. Say what you do in plain terms. Avoid puffed-up adjectives. Don't sell around the thing—just say the thing.

That includes your social proof.

A testimonial that says, "They revolutionized our operations and exceeded every expectation" is far less effective than one that says, "We saw a 38% drop in onboarding time within three months."

Specificity beats superlatives every time. It feels real. It makes people believe.

This is also where the format of your copy matters. Long walls of text make even strong content feel harder to trust. When something looks difficult to read, we assume it's going to be difficult to understand. So we skip it. And if we skip too much of a page, we lose context—and when we lose context, trust suffers.

Breaking up your copy visually can have just as much impact as rewriting it. Think of your paragraphs as moments of clarity. Each one should make one point, clearly. If you have five ideas in a single paragraph, split them. Let each idea stand on its own.

And let people find their way to it naturally.

That's why layout supports credibility. If someone lands mid-scroll and their eyes fall on a concise testimonial, a short proof point, or a single strong sentence, they're more likely to pause. More likely to engage. More likely to keep going.

You're not just earning trust through what you say. You're earning it through how you say it. How you structure it. How easy it is to consume.

This isn't about dumbing it down. It's about leveling the field.

You're not writing for a less intelligent reader. You're writing for a busy one. A skeptical one. A reader who has 20 tabs open and isn't going to reward your nuance unless your clarity earns their attention first.

Because clarity is not just a signal of good writing. It's a signal of good thinking. And good thinking builds trust faster than any clever tagline ever will.

So instead of trying to sound important, try to sound true.

Say what you do. Show how it works. Back it up with something real. And let the visitor decide.

That's what credible companies do. They don't push harder. They pull more clearly.

The Power of Proof: What You Say Isn't Enough

Every brand claims they're the best. Every product promises results. Every agency says they care. That's why what *you* say about your business will never matter as much as what others say about it.

Proof is the bridge between your claims and your credibility.

And it's not just about stacking testimonials at the bottom of the page. Real proof is integrated. It's layered into the story. It shows up right when the visitor needs a little push—a moment of doubt, hesitation, or curiosity.

If you say your product is easy to use, show a customer quote saying they had it up and running in five minutes. Better yet, show them a video. If you claim your service saves businesses time or makes them more money, give them a real-world example or a case study that quantifies it. Don't just assert—demonstrate.

That's why great proof isn't one-size-fits-all. It comes in different forms, and each plays a unique role depending on where the visitor is in their journey.

A testimonial makes your claims feel real, especially when it mentions specific outcomes or addresses real concerns. A case study adds depth. It shows the thinking, the process, and the results, giving visitors a fuller picture of what it's like to work with you. Recognizable client logos or media mentions create immediate surface-level trust, even before someone reads a word of your copy. Ratings and reviews, especially those with photos or clear detail, can be incredibly persuasive for products. They're social proof in volume. And then there's visual proof: before-

and-after images, screenshots, demo videos. These often do more than any paragraph could ever say.

These various forms of proof aren't just persuasive tactics; they also provide tangible evidence for the E-E-A-T factors that Google's raters look for. Compelling case studies and specific testimonials demonstrate real-world Experience (E) and Expertise (E). Recognizable client logos or media features contribute to Authoritativeness (A). Positive reviews build Trustworthiness (T) and contribute to the site's overall reputation, another key consideration in the quality guidelines.

Resist the urge to fake what you may not have. One specific, grounded quote is more powerful than a dozen vague blurbs from your best friends or employees. Visitors can smell fluff a mile away. If it feels staged or hollow, it'll do more harm than good.

But when proof is authentic, specific, and well-timed, it creates momentum. It softens resistance. Visitors stop wondering *if* they can trust you and start asking themselves *what if this actually works for me too?*

That's when trust stops being passive—and starts turning into action.

Signals That Build Trust on Every Page

Trust doesn't live in a single section of your site. It's not something you slap onto the footer or tuck into a testimonial carousel. It's built—or lost—on every scroll, click, and pause.

That means every page needs to carry its own weight when it comes to trust.

It starts with consistency. If your homepage looks sleek and modern but your product or service pages feel like they were written in a rush, visitors notice. It doesn't matter how convincing the copy is if the visual quality drops halfway through the journey.

Inconsistency makes people second-guess.

Even subtle things—like mismatched buttons, broken links, or outdated copyright years—can raise quiet red flags.

You might not think they matter. Your visitor does. Even if they don't realize it. Their actions are affected by those little details.

We already covered your copy but also consider your tone. Does it sound like it was written by a real person? Does it feel confident without sounding arrogant, helpful without sounding desperate?

When your messaging strikes the right tone—one that's aligned with your brand but grounded in your visitor's reality—it builds a sense of rapport. It's subtle, but powerful. The moment someone *feels* like you "get it," you start to build rapport.

You want to make sure that your visual cues maintain that rapport. Clean, uncluttered design. Responsive layout. Mobile optimization. Fast load times.

These things don't just help usability—they signal professionalism. A slow, janky site makes people nervous.

Then there's transparency. Clear pricing. Clear policies. Clear expectations. If you hide the cost or bury important details in fine print, people will assume the worst.

Trust grows when there's nothing to hide. That means showing your process. Explaining what happens next. Giving people reasons to feel confident that when they take action, they're not walking into the unknown.

Service businesses especially benefit from this. The more personal the offering, the more the visitor wants to know who they're dealing with. That's where team pages, bios, and even behind-the-scenes content can carry real weight.

It's not fluff—it's reassurance.

For eCommerce, this often means product-specific detail: shipping info that's easy to find, return policies that are simple and fair, photos that show the real product from every angle.

You're not just selling the product. You're selling the *experience* of buying it. If that experience feels trustworthy, people will follow through.

But here's the truth: even with all the right elements in place, trust is fragile. One confusing moment, one mixed message, one broken promise, and it can vanish.

That's why trust-building has to be a system, not a feature. It's something you design for at every level of the site.

Because people don't convert when they're convinced. They convert when they're comfortable.

And nothing creates comfort like a site that *feels* trustworthy from the first click to the last.

Trust doesn't happen when you say the right words. It happens when you show up consistently—when your message, your visuals, your tone, and your experience all line up and feel real.

Visitors don't need you to be perfect. They just need you to make sense. To feel credible. To feel clear.

That kind of trust isn't built through cleverness or flash. It's built by seeing the site through their eyes, and removing everything that makes them hesitate.

Because when a site *feels* trustworthy, people don't just stick around. They lean in.

And that's when real conversion begins.

Making It Make Sense: Giving Visitors the Right Context

Even if your visuals are strong and your tone is dialed in, the message still falls flat if it doesn't make sense.

Clarity isn't just about content, it's also about context. Your visitor has to understand what they're looking at, why it matters, and how it fits into their decision-making process.

Too many websites assume too much. They assume the visitor already knows who they are, what the product does, or why their service is different. But that's rarely the case.

People land on your site in all kinds of ways—from Google searches, social media, ads, emails, or random links. Some know you well. Others have never heard of you.

Your copy needs to meet them where they are.

That's why context is everything. It's what bridges the gap between what you know and what your visitor knows. And it's what keeps your message from sounding like it was dropped in from nowhere.

For example, let's say you sell sustainable running shoes. A homepage headline that says "Built for Impact" might sound punchy, but without context, it's meaningless. Impact how? On your joints? On the planet? On performance?

Now imagine the headline said, "Sustainable performance shoes designed to go the distance." Instantly, there's context: what the product is, who it's for, and why it matters.

That's the difference. Context turns copy into communication.

This becomes especially important when you're selling something unfamiliar. Maybe your service uses a new model people haven't seen before. Maybe your product does something traditional options don't. Maybe it solves a problem your visitors don't even know they have.

That's where clarity and context work together. You can't just name the thing—you have to situate it in a story they understand.

A lot of businesses skip this step because they're too close to the offer.

You've been in the weeds. You know your feature set, your differentiators, your value prop. But your visitors don't. And they don't care, until you show them why they should.

That doesn't mean you need to write paragraphs of backstory. It just means you need to create small bridges. Add a few words that explain what something is or why it matters. Introduce a section with a sentence that tells the reader why they should keep going. Drop in a quick comparison to help people understand your product in familiar terms.

These aren't filler lines—they're friction reducers.

For eCommerce, this might mean explaining why your premium shaving kit costs three times more than the drugstore version. Maybe you talk about the materials. Maybe you focus on the experience. Maybe you highlight the lifetime guarantee. But you can't just show the price and hope the customer connects the dots. The context is what makes the price feel justified.

For service businesses, it might be explaining what happens after someone fills out the contact form. "We'll follow up within 24 hours" is better than nothing. "You'll get a short questionnaire to help us understand your goals, followed by a free 30-minute strategy call" is even better.

It removes the mystery. It builds confidence. And it makes that next step feel easier.

Ultimately, when people hesitate, it's often because they're missing context. Something doesn't quite click. Something feels disconnected. They don't know where they are in the journey or what happens next.

Focus on that. Guide them. Fill in the gaps. Do that and you won't just earn trust—you build a site that performs.

And as you've figured out by now, that's exactly what Google rewards. In the next chapter, we'll look at how search engines evaluate your site, and why the same principles that help users convert are the ones that help you rank.

Chapter 7:
SEO That Actually Works

Why User-Focused SEO Wins Now

There's a reason most SEO advice feels outdated the second you apply it. That's because the world of search has changed—but the way people talk about it hasn't.

Old-school SEO was all about keywords, hacks, and checklists. Sprinkle your focus phrase three times in the first paragraph. Make sure your title has the exact match. Update your meta description and keywords. Add some backlinks, stuff a few more phrases in the footer, and boom—you're on page one.

That game is over. Or at least, it's irrelevant to anyone building a real business.

Today, SEO isn't about keyword density. It's about usefulness. Clarity. Speed. Relevance.

It's about how well your site satisfies the intent behind a search, and how confidently it helps the visitor get what they came for. Because that's what Google is optimizing for now. Not technical trickery. Not textbook "optimization." But actual *helpfulness*.

Google's entire ranking system is now centered around user satisfaction. That's not speculation—it's in the documentation.

The "Helpful Content" update (Google it) wasn't just a nudge. It was a shift in how quality is defined. Helpful isn't optional anymore. It's the new baseline.

Pages are evaluated based on whether they fulfill the *purpose* behind a query. Whether they meet expectations, build trust, and demonstrate experience.

News flash: keywords, once the whole foundation behind a successful SEO strategy, are almost irrelevant.

If you've been following along with this book, this should sound familiar.

Google's vision of a high-quality website overlaps almost perfectly with what real users want: fast, clear, relevant content that feels trustworthy and easy to use.

So here's the good news: If you build a great website—one that's structured well, answers real questions, and flows naturally—you're already doing better SEO than half the sites trying to game the system.

You don't need to out-hack your competition. You need to out-help them.

That's not to say keywords don't matter. They do—but not in the way most people think.

The point of using a keyword isn't to "rank." It's to signal relevance. If someone searches "best invoicing software for freelancers," they're not looking for a generic page that just says "invoicing software" fifty times. They're looking for a clear, helpful answer.

Something written in plain language that speaks to them like a human. Something that demonstrates expertise without sounding robotic. Something that feels like the right result.

Sure, in most cases that will include the keyword, but that's not the reason it's ranking - it's because it satisfies the intent of the searcher.

This is why bounce rate, time on site, and even user engagement metrics (like clicking deeper into the site) are quietly shaping your rankings.

If someone lands on your page and bounces right back to Google, that sends a signal. So does how many people are clicking on your result instead of others.

That's not "SEO voodoo." That's search engines doing their job—ranking based on what people *actually prefer*.

Google sees everything. They know exactly how long it takes someone to come back after clicking a result—and if that return happens quickly, it's a signal that the first page didn't deliver. When enough people bounce back like that, the ranking drops.

On the flip side, if users stick around, that's a strong vote of confidence. And Google adjusts accordingly.

So, what does this mean for you?

It means SEO isn't a separate project. It's not a checklist at the end of a build. It's something baked into the foundation of your website.

If you're already focused on clarity, helpfulness, and a good user experience, you're already halfway there.

But if you've been designing for aesthetics first and hoping SEO gets tacked on later, you're setting yourself up to lose.

SEO today isn't about beating the algorithm. It's about winning the visitor.

Because when your site does that—when it loads fast, reads clearly, and gives people what they came for—Google notices. And rewards you accordingly.

That's where we'll start.

In the next section, we'll look at the technical basics that actually matter, and which common SEO "must-haves" are wildly overrated.

How Search Intent Shapes the Page

Every strong-performing page on your site should have two jobs: it needs to serve your audience, and it needs to satisfy search intent.

When those two things align, good things happen. But when they're out of sync, even by a little, Google knows. And your visitors do too.

Search intent is what someone *actually* wants when they type something into Google. Not just the words they used, but the goal behind the search.

Are they looking to learn? To compare? To buy? To solve a problem? Your page needs to answer that question, clearly and directly.

Let's say someone searches for "best email marketing platforms." That's a commercial intent query. They're not trying to learn what email marketing is—they're trying to decide between options.

A blog post that explains the history of email marketing or breaks down every possible use case will likely miss the mark. What they really want is a list of platforms, with pros, cons, pricing, maybe some comparison tables, and a clear recommendation.

Now imagine they search "how to improve email open rates." That's informational intent. They're looking to learn, not to buy.

So if they land on a product page for your email tool, with no tips or guidance, you've just lost them. The page may be great, but not for *that* person in *that* moment.

This mismatch happens all the time. Companies create content they think will rank, but they don't stop to ask: what is the searcher actually trying to do? So they write blog posts that are too salesy or product pages that are too vague. And then they wonder why the traffic doesn't convert, or why the rankings don't stick.

Google's gotten scary good at detecting intent mismatches.

If a user hits your page and bounces quickly, that sends a strong "Needs Not Met" signal. And you don't get many chances to fix it.

So how do you make sure your content aligns with intent?

Start by looking at what's already ranking.

If you're targeting a keyword like "accounting software for freelancers," and the top results are all comparison guides and listicles, don't try to rank with a straight product page.

Google's showing you what searchers expect. Fight that pattern, and you're swimming upstream. Follow it and improve on it, and you've got a shot.

Next, ask: what does someone need to believe or understand in order to take the next step?

If they're in research mode, give them clarity. If they're in buying mode, make the path obvious. And if they're somewhere in between, help them navigate the rest of the journey.

Intent also influences your layout.

For informational content, you might want to include internal links to deeper resources. For commercial intent, quick-scan comparison blocks, buyer checklists, and light CTAs can all help the reader move forward. And for transactional pages, the goal is to minimize distraction—clarity, focus, and action.

One more thing: don't try to serve every intent on a single page. That's how you end up with content that's bloated, confused, and underperforming.

It's okay to have different pages for different intents. In fact, that's how you build a structure that works—for search engines and for people.

Because when you match your page to the reader's mindset, they stay. They engage. They convert.

And Google takes notice.

At the same time, you want to make sure that you watch out for duplication.

This happens when two or more pages serve essentially the same purpose or cover the same topic. Maybe you have a "Services" page that describes your offerings, and then separate pages that do the same thing, but with slightly different wording. Or maybe you have two blog posts targeting nearly identical search terms.

The problem here is twofold:

1. You're splitting your visibility and authority between multiple pages
2. You're confusing your visitors. They don't know where to go, so they hesitate—or worse, they bounce.

Google also sees this as a problem.

It's called cannibalization. When two pages compete for the same topic, neither one wins. Instead of one strong result, you have two weaker ones.

Google's quality guidelines specifically address content duplication, noting it can be characteristic of lower-quality sites as it confuses users and search engines alike, potentially diluting the site's perceived authority

The fix is consolidation. Combine overlapping content into a single, stronger page. Redirect the weaker ones.

Clean up the mess and focus your authority.

Page Structure That Helps (Not Hurts) Your Rankings

There's a persistent myth that SEO is mostly about keywords. Sprinkle in the right phrases, hit some word count, and voilà—you're on the first page.

It used to be like that in the 90s... but modern SEO doesn't work that way. Especially not for competitive terms.

Today, structure matters just as much as content.

If your page is hard to parse, clunky to scan, or confusing to navigate, it won't matter how good your copy is. You'll lose users. And when you lose users, Google takes that as a sign your page didn't deliver.

Good structure helps people *and* search engines find what they're looking for—fast.

At a basic level, that means using clear, consistent heading levels. Not just for visual hierarchy, but for actual content organization.

Google reads your H1s, H2s, and H3s to understand what the page is about. If your headings don't reflect the real content underneath—or worse, if they're missing altogether—you're leaving search engines (and visitors) guessing.

Don't get it twisted - I'm not saying that your main keyword must be your H1, and that you must have related keywords as H2s.

These "rules" that many SEO companies live by are not really what it's all about today, and I challenge you to see if all the first results for strong competitive keywords follow them.

They don't. Some do, and some don't. Because it doesn't always make sense, and it can feel spammy.

What I am saying is that you should give each page one clear topic, and that topic should be evident through your biggest heading - in code that biggest heading is typically labeled H1, so a properly coded website would label it as such. That's all.

Don't try to rank a single post for ten different keyword clusters by cramming every variation into every paragraph. That just dilutes your message.

Instead, give each page one job, and link to related pages where it makes sense. That helps your internal architecture and spreads your relevance across the site.

And speaking of internal links, use them. Thoughtfully. Don't rely on generic "read more" links or dump them all into the footer. Guide your visitor deeper. Link to pages that expand the conversation or answer the next logical question.

If someone lands on a blog post about hiring a developer, link them to your dev team services. If they're on a comparison guide, link them to your pricing page.

That kind of structure tells both users and Google that your site is connected, organized, and trustworthy.

Now let's talk about navigation.

Your nav is not a dumping ground for every page on your site. It's a strategic tool. Keep it focused. We've talked about this already in the context of user experience, but from an SEO perspective, the same rule applies with even more weight.

Use labels that match what your audience actually searches for. If they're looking for "pricing," don't hide it under "plans." If your key service is "content strategy," don't bury it under "solutions."

Make your nav mirror the language and priorities of your ideal customer. That helps users orient quickly—and it tells Google what you're about.

Then there's URL structure.

Keep it clean. Keep it readable. Avoid numbers, filler words, and endless nested folders. A URL like /services/seo-consulting is easier to understand—for humans and search engine bots—than something like /our-solutions/digital_001/page?id=1732.

Even technical elements, like how your pages are tagged and grouped, influence how Google crawls and indexes your site.

If your category pages are thin, or your tags are messy, you're not just wasting *crawl budget*—you're sending mixed signals about what matters.

Google isn't going to spend hours trying to decode your site, and neither are your visitors. They will both spend some time on it, and that's all you get.

For Google we call this your "crawl budget", and for visitors it's their attention span. Use that limited attention wisely. Link to your most important pages often, and do it in a way that naturally guides people (and bots) to what matters next.

Good structure is good SEO, but more importantly, it's good design. It's what makes people stay, explore, and trust.

But structure isn't just about helping Google. It's about reducing effort for your visitors.

A well-structured page gives people confidence. It makes the experience feel intentional. And when everything flows logically—when each section answers a question or clears up a doubt—it makes users stick around longer.

Which is exactly what Google wants to see.

So yes, you still want solid content. Yes, you still need to target the right topics. But if your structure doesn't support the experience, you're building on shaky ground.

Don't let sloppy structure drag your rankings down.

Build pages that are as easy to navigate as they are to read. Use your layout to reinforce clarity. And make sure everything, from your headings to your links to your nav, is working together to support the page's goal.

Because great SEO isn't just about writing.

It's about shaping the entire experience so it clicks—for the visitor *and* the algorithm.

Use this worksheet to identify potential overlaps on your site and plan consolidation or refocusing efforts.

Step 1: List the main topics, services, products, or keyword themes.

Step 2: Identify the *single best page* that should target it (Primary Target Page).

Step 3: List any *other pages* that also significantly cover the same topic or target very similar keywords.

Core Topic / Keyword Theme	Primary Target Page	Other Competing Page

Now here's your big question:

Do the competing pages have a truly distinct angle, purpose, or target a different intent stage?

If the answer is **no,** then you have 3 choices

- Consolidate into the primary target.
- Refocus the competing page(s) on more specific keywords.
- Delete and/or redirect the redundant competing pages(s).

Content That Ranks (And Deserves To)

You can't fake your way onto page one anymore. Not for anything that matters.

That's the real shift in modern SEO. Google's not just looking for content that matches the query. It's looking for content that *satisfies* it. Content that feels complete. That answers the right questions. That respects the user's time and gives them what they came for, faster and better than the rest.

The best way to think about SEO content in 2025? Don't try to rank—try to *deserve* to rank.

The strongest-performing content doesn't just check boxes. It earns its spot by being useful, clear, original, and aligned with intent. And it's not about length—it's about impact.

Some of the top-ranking pages on Google are long. Some are short. Some are loaded with visuals. Others are plain. The difference isn't the format. It's the quality of the thinking behind it.

The ones that win are the ones that answer questions completely, communicate clearly, and leave the user feeling like they've found what they were looking for.

Let's talk about that idea of "complete."

It doesn't mean stuffing every possible keyword variation into the page. It means covering a topic thoroughly and naturally—anticipating what someone might still be wondering, and building that into the flow. That might mean expanding on related topics, showing examples, adding diagrams, or linking out to deeper resources.

Here's the test: when someone finishes reading your page, *are they done searching*?

If not—if they bounce back to Google to keep looking—you didn't satisfy their intent. And Google tracks that. Every time. It uses that to identify patterns to reward the sites that do good, or penalize those that don't.

This is especially true with informational content like blog posts, guides, and how-to pages. The old playbook was: pick a keyword, write 800 words, and move on.

But now, the bar is higher. Because competition is higher. Everyone's playing the same game, and the internet is flooded with reworded summaries of the same top five search results.

So the pages that rise to the top are the ones that add something new.

That might be original research. Personal experience. Data nobody else has. A sharper way of explaining something complex. A comparison that nobody's framed quite like you.

Google doesn't need 10 rewrites of the same article—it needs the one that's actually best.

And "best" doesn't mean fancy. It means helpful.

Clarity wins. Relevance wins. Even formatting can help you win.

Use proper headings to break things up. Add bullets where it makes sense. Call out definitions. Include a TL;DR at the top for longer pieces. These aren't "SEO tricks"—they're reading enhancements. They make your content easier to use. And Google wants to rank the pages that are easiest to use.

If you're not sure where to start, here's a simple question to ask: what's something your customer is trying to figure out, but nobody's explained well?

Write *that* page.

Do it better than the rest.

Not longer. Better.

And then make absolutely sure that page is part of your site's internal structure. Link to it from related services. Feature it in your resource center. Make it findable.

The best content in the world doesn't help if it's buried three layers deep and never connected to your main journey.

The same logic applies to landing pages, service pages, and product descriptions.

Every page is a chance to solve a problem, answer a question, or help someone make a decision. That's what makes it valuable to the visitor—and to Google.

The goal isn't just to get clicks. It's to earn trust. To show your expertise. To move someone closer to what they came for.

If your content can do that—consistently, clearly, and with real usefulness—then rankings follow.

Because Google doesn't just rank content that's optimized. It ranks content that works.

Backlinks:
The Shortcut You Sometimes Need

Let's get something out of the way: I hate backlinks.

Not because they don't work. They do. But because they feel like a dated workaround. Like a relic from the early internet that we haven't evolved past.

In a perfect world, great content would be enough. You'd publish something truly valuable, and if it helped people, it would rise on its own merits. That's the future.

Platforms like TikTok already work that way. You don't need the most followers to get views. You just need a great piece of content. Smaller accounts go viral every day, because the algorithm is built to surface quality over legacy.

But the web isn't TikTok. Not just yet.

Google still has to sift through millions of pages all trying to rank for the same topics. And in that noise, it leans on signals.

Backlinks are one of the strongest signals. When one site links to another, it's seen as a vote of confidence. The more quality sites linking to you, the more Google starts to trust you.

So even though it shouldn't matter—it does. Especially for newer sites that haven't built that trust yet.

You could have the best article in your industry, but if your domain is brand new and your competitor has a five-year head start and hundreds of backlinks, they're probably going to outrank you. At least for a while.

That's the harsh reality.

Backlinks don't guarantee quality. But they do fast-track trust.

And in SEO, trust gets you seen.

So how do you actually get backlinks? There are dozens of tactics, but they tend to fall into a few main buckets:

1. **Earned (Organic) backlinks.** These are the good ones. Someone finds your content helpful and links to it organically—from a blog post, a newsletter, a forum, or even a press article. This happens naturally when your content is actually useful. But it also takes time. And patience.
2. **Outreach backlinks.** These come from sending cold emails to website owners, journalists, or bloggers and asking them to link to your page. Sometimes you pitch a specific article. Sometimes you offer to write a guest post. It can work, but it's a grind, and unless your content is *truly* worth linking to, most people will ignore you.
3. **Strategic backlinks.** These come from partnerships. Maybe you sponsor a conference, and they link back to your site. Maybe a vendor lists you as a recommended provider. Maybe you collaborate on content with another brand. These links are usually higher quality and more relevant—but they require relationships, not just emails.
4. **Paid backlinks.** This is the "dark side" of SEO. Everybody is doing it, but almost nobody is proud of it. Here is what Google officially says "Any links intended to manipulate PageRank or a site's ranking in Google search results may be considered part of a link scheme and a violation of Google's Spam Policies."

Google hates paid backlinks because they're meant to be a vote of confidence and not a commodity you can buy. But everybody does. So let's talk about it.

The best type of backlink is one that comes from a reputable source that is also directly related to your topic.

For example, if I'm a business school then getting a link from Harvard is possibly the best I could get. Getting a link from a regional business school is still very good, because it's related, even though it's not very reputable. Getting a link from a small local newspaper is decent, because it's geographically relevant, even if it's not topic-specific or especially authoritative. Getting a link from a random Pinterest profile about flowers is worth almost nothing, since it's not related nor reputable.

It's more complicated than that, but this is a fairly simple and accurate way to evaluate the value of a backlink.

Want to go one layer deeper? Then look at how difficult it is to actually earn the link.

For example, anyone could make a Facebook page and link to their website in a few minutes. Anyone could leave a comment on a blog or a reply on Reddit and link to their website. Let's step it up a bit. Many people could post a free (or cheap) Press Release and get it distributed on a few hundred websites about their company, giving them a few hundred links. All of these links are worth very little, because they're very easy to get, and Google knows that.

On the flipside, very few websites will ever get links from Wikipedia, or a government website, or an editorial write up on a big magazine.

These links are worth a ton. They are difficult—even impossible—to buy.

And yet, you can still go on Fiverr right now and buy 100+ links for $5, from spammy blog comments, private link farms, or automated syndication.

These types of links have not worked in many years, but people still sell them because many still buy them. Don't be one of those people.

If you're going to buy backlinks, which I'm not officially endorsing since it's against the rules, then do it in such a way so that you can get the most exclusive links that your money can buy, and focus on links that make sense naturally.

If you're a local plumber then it doesn't make sense for you to have a Wikipedia page. It doesn't look right.

But maybe you could have a writeup in the local trade newspaper. This would be very beneficial since your audience and your whole business depends on locality. It also looks natural.

If you're an apparel brand, then how cool would it be if your products were listed in seasonal guides from reputable industry publications?

That's how you should think. Reputable, related, and exclusive.

So where does that leave us?

Backlinks are like kindling. They help you get the fire started. But if the fire doesn't catch, if the content sucks, or your site experience is weak, then it won't matter.

You'll get the click, and you'll lose it just as fast.

Here's the smarter approach: build a site that actually deserves backlinks. Then pick a few high-value pieces of content—ones that are genuinely helpful, clearly written, and well-structured—and focus your outreach there.

Ask partners to link. Share it in your industry's newsletters. Mention it when you're a guest on a podcast. Give people a reason to share it.

Don't chase backlinks. Earn them. Strategically.

Because while backlinks might give you a boost, they're only valuable if the content behind them can hold attention.

And that's where you win.

Chapter 8:
Performance That Actually Feels Fast

Site Speed - What Visitors Actually Notice

When people talk about website speed, they usually focus on numbers—load time, performance scores, Lighthouse audits, and Core Web Vitals.

But real users don't think in metrics. They don't sit there with a stopwatch. They just feel whether your site is fast…or not.

That's the key: perceived performance is what matters. And perceived performance is often wildly different from actual load time.

You can have a page that technically loads in under two seconds, but if it feels sluggish—if there's a delay between click and response, if things jump around as they settle into place, or if it just takes too long for the important stuff to show up—your visitor experiences it as slow.

On the flip side, a site might take five seconds to fully load, but if it shows something useful right away, reacts instantly to taps and scrolls, and guides the visitor smoothly through the experience, it *feels* fast.

That feeling is everything.

Because "slow" isn't just about waiting. It's about uncertainty.

When a site lags or glitches, the visitor starts wondering: Did my click register? Is this broken? Am I wasting my time?

That tiny moment of doubt breaks trust. And if it happens in the first few seconds, it can kill the visit entirely.

So yes, speed matters.

But not in the way most people think. The goal isn't to win a race—it's to remove friction. To make the experience feel smooth, responsive, and under control.

That's what people notice. That's what makes them stay. And that's what we'll focus on in this chapter.

Smoothing the Experience (Without Obsessing Over Scores)

Even though speed is invisible, friction is not.

Visitors won't notice if your site loads in 2.3 seconds instead of 3.1, but they'll absolutely notice if your page jumps around as it loads, or if they tap a button and nothing happens for a few beats.

That's why the goal isn't to chase a perfect score. It's to eliminate the little moments of resistance that make your site feel sluggish—even if, technically, it's fine.

The easiest way to start is by actually using your site like a real visitor. Load it on your phone. Try it on a slower Wi-Fi connection. Click around as if you were shopping or considering a service. Look for the cracks.

Where does it stall? Where does it feel weirdly slow, even if the numbers say otherwise? Where does a small hiccup break the flow?

That's the difference between performance and perception. It's not about milliseconds—it's about momentum.

You might notice something simple, like a page that loads quickly but feels slow because the fonts pop in late. Or a contact form that takes a few seconds to validate and submit, with no visual cue to let the user know anything is happening.

These are small delays, but they stack up, and they leave people guessing.

Here's where tools can help, but only if you use them with the right mindset.

Tools like Google PageSpeed Insights, GTmetrix, or WebPageTest can surface helpful clues. They might flag images that are too big, scripts that load inefficiently, or third-party tools that slow things down. That's all good input.

But these tools aren't user experience simulators—they're diagnostic reports. They don't know your audience, and they don't understand context. They just measure what's happening behind the scenes.

So don't obsess over the score. A low score doesn't always mean a bad experience. A high score doesn't always mean a good one. A site that gets a C+ from Lighthouse but feels fast to users is winning. A site that gets an A+ but annoys visitors with jumpy layout shifts or delayed interactions is still failing.

Here's an example: Let's say your product page has a large photo carousel halfway down. The images are heavy, so the page technically doesn't "finish" loading for several seconds.

PageSpeed Insights flags this, and your score drops. But here's the thing—the user doesn't need those images right away. If they're still engaging with the top of the page—reading a headline, watching a quick video, or choosing a size—the images can quietly load in the background. As long as they're ready by the time the user scrolls, there's no issue. In fact, it can feel fast.

That's why your performance strategy should be shaped by how your users behave—not just by what a tool says.

Start by fixing the things your visitors actually notice.

If the layout shifts and makes a button jump just as someone is about to click it, that's a problem. If the "Add to Cart" button takes too long to react after a tap, or if an image at the top takes a second too long to load, that's a red flag. If your popup blocks the screen before the content finishes loading, or your form has no visual cue to show it's submitting, that's friction. And friction kills flow.

Most of these aren't technical performance issues. They're user experience problems. And the user experience is what determines whether someone stays or leaves.

An eCommerce brand we worked with had a "quick view" feature for products on their collection pages. On slower collections, it lagged because the modal was trying to load all product images before opening. It took about two seconds to appear after a tap—long enough that users often tapped again, thinking nothing had happened. That second tap led to frustration, misclicks, and abandoned sessions.

We didn't overhaul the feature. We simply reworked the modal so it would open as soon as the first image loaded. The rest of the images kept loading in the background.

The actual load time didn't change, but now the interaction felt responsive. It felt like progress. And that feeling made all the difference.

That's the shift. You're not trying to win a race. You're trying to create smooth, fluid, low-resistance experiences that keep people moving forward without hesitation.

Focus on what feels slow. Because that's what visitors remember. If it's annoying to interact with, they won't care that your Lighthouse score is a 97.

In the next section, we'll look at how to intentionally design that sense of flow—using visual cues, animations, and interactive moments to make your site feel faster, even when it's not.

Speed As A Trust Signal

A fast-feeling site doesn't just create a better experience.

It communicates something deeper: this business is competent. This brand has its act together. I can trust these people.

That may sound dramatic, but it's how human psychology works online. When everything flows—when buttons respond instantly, images appear right when you expect them, and the page doesn't jump around—you stop noticing the site. You just move.

And that smoothness creates confidence.

On the flip side, slowness—even tiny moments of it—creates doubt. A button that takes too long to respond makes you wonder if it's broken. A page that stutters as it loads makes you question if the company is cutting corners. A form that hangs after you submit it makes you second-guess the whole interaction.

These aren't rational thoughts. They're gut reactions. But they stick.

Because online, trust is fragile. The visitor doesn't know you. They can't see your office or meet your team.

All they have is your website, and the way it behaves becomes a stand-in for how your business operates.

This is especially true on mobile. If your site chugs or jitters, even a little, it feels like an afterthought. But when it glides, when it feels light and responsive, it gives the impression of care, quality, and professionalism.

And that perception builds trust—before you've said a single word.

That's why speed isn't just a usability issue. It's a branding issue. It's not about shaving milliseconds off a load time just to impress Google. It's about removing resistance so your visitors can focus on what matters: your offer, your message, your product.

The best part? When your site feels fast, people are more patient. They're more forgiving. They scroll longer. They explore more. They convert more.

Because in a world where most sites are clunky and chaotic, smoothness is a signal. It says: you care.

And when visitors feel that, they stay. They buy. They trust.

That's the power of real performance. Not just speed—but ease, momentum, and confidence.

But performance isn't a one-time fix. It's a moving target. Browsers change. Devices evolve. Expectations shift.

In the next chapter, we'll explore how to keep your site sharp over time, by refining instead of redesigning, and improving what matters without starting from scratch.

Performance Friction Audit Checklist

Test your key website pages and answer honestly:
(especially on mobile and simulate a slower connection if possible)

1. **Overall Feel:** Does navigating the site generally feel smooth and responsive, or are there noticeable pauses or moments where it seems to stall?

2. **Layout Shift During Load:** As pages load, do images, ads, or other content blocks cause the layout to visibly jump or rearrange significantly, potentially causing misclicks?

3. **Interaction Lag:** When you tap or click on primary buttons (like 'Add to Cart', navigation links, submit buttons), is there a noticeable delay before the site visually responds or acknowledges the action?

4. **Font Loading:** Do you notice text appearing briefly in a standard system font before switching to the site's actual chosen web font (sometimes called a "flash of unstyled text" or FOUT)?

5. **Form Submission Feedback:** When submitting forms (contact, checkout, etc.), is there immediate and clear visual feedback indicating that the submission is processing (e.g., a spinner, a "Submitting..." message)?

6. **Popup/Overlay Timing:** If using popups or overlays (for newsletters, special offers, etc.), do they ever appear *before* the main, essential content of the page has loaded and become usable?

7. **Complex Component Speed:** Do interactive elements like image sliders/carousels, complex menus, or "quick view" modals load and respond quickly, or do they feel sluggish?

8. **Mobile Experience:** Specifically on a mobile device, do any of the above issues feel significantly worse or more frustrating compared to desktop?

9. **Consistency:** Is the *feeling* of performance consistent across different types of pages (homepage, product/service pages, blog posts), or do some sections feel noticeably slower than others?

Chapter 9:
The Best Sites Keep Evolving

Don't Redesign–Refine

The moment most people realize their website isn't working the way they want, their instinct is to start over. Scrap the whole thing. Burn it down and rebuild from scratch.

That instinct makes sense. When something feels broken—or just stale—it's easy to assume it needs a full reset.

But the truth is, most underperforming websites don't need a full redesign. They need refinement. Small, strategic changes that fix what's not working without tossing out the parts that are.

Redesigning from scratch is expensive. It's time-consuming. And it comes with risk—because unless your strategy has evolved dramatically, you'll likely end up rebuilding the same problems in a prettier wrapper.

The layout might change. The colors might shift. But if the messaging is still vague, the structure still unclear, or the user journey still clunky, you've just spent months (and tens of thousands of dollars) to make something look newer, not work better.

Instead of chasing a fresh coat of paint, start by asking better questions. What's actually broken? What's causing friction? Where are visitors dropping off? What assumptions are baked into your current site that might no longer be true?

You don't need to fix what isn't broken.

Maybe your structure is solid, but your copy feels generic. Maybe your hero section works, but your product pages are missing urgency. Maybe your CTAs aren't positioned for the right level of intent. These are refinements—not reinventions.

And refining doesn't just save time and money. It sharpens your focus.

It forces you to look at your site with a critical, strategic lens instead of being distracted by the surface. You're not chasing novelty. You're making your site measurably better.

We've seen brands triple their conversion rates just by tightening their headlines, simplifying their navigation, and fixing one clunky interaction on mobile.

No rebrand. No rebuild. Just thoughtful iteration.

Actively maintaining and improving your site also sends positive signals about its ongoing care and relevance, contributing to perceptions of E-E-A-T.

In fact, Google's quality guidelines specifically note the importance of maintaining accurate and up-to-date information, especially for pages dealing with significant topics.

That's what high-performing websites do. They don't throw everything out when something feels off—they improve it. They treat the site like a product, not a poster. Something you evolve, not something you start over every two years.

And that shift in mindset is everything. Because the moment you stop seeing your website as a fixed project and start seeing it as a living part of your business, you give yourself permission to evolve.

Not in one big splash, but in steady, intentional moves that build momentum and results.

How to Make Smart Changes

Great websites aren't built in one go—they're built over time.

The most successful businesses know that a site is never really "done." It's a living part of your brand, and the smartest teams treat it like one.

That means instead of constantly redesigning, they make focused, strategic refinements. They look for what's working, what's not, and what could be better. Then they act with precision.

The first step is to stop thinking of updates as big events. You don't need a six-month redesign project to move the needle. Sometimes, a single change can drive real results. One updated headline. One clearer value prop. One tighter CTA.

These small changes compound, and they're often easier to measure, easier to implement, and less risky than massive overhauls.

Let's say you notice that visitors are bouncing from your pricing page. That's not a reason to redesign the whole site. It's a prompt to ask better questions. Are the prices unclear? Is the value not obvious? Are people missing key differentiators that justify the cost? Maybe a short explainer video or a visual comparison chart could help.

You don't need a new design system. You need better communication, right where the friction exists.

We once worked with a SaaS brand that had a stunning homepage but wanted to improve their conversions. The structure was clean, the layout modern—but the message was off.

The hero section said "Unlock the Future of Workflow Intelligence." That sounds impressive, but it doesn't mean anything concrete. We changed it to something dead simple: "Automate repetitive tasks with one-click integrations." Conversions jumped 28%. No layout changes. Just better clarity.

That's the power of focused refinements. They allow you to preserve everything that's working while zeroing in on what's not.

It's not just more efficient. It's more respectful to your users. Instead of making them relearn a whole new interface or navigation system, you're improving the experience they already know.

Another example: an eCommerce brand we worked with saw that mobile users were dropping off right before checkout. On review, we saw that the "Proceed to Checkout" button was buried under a collapsed summary of cart items. On desktop, this wasn't a problem. But on mobile, it created just enough friction to cause hesitation.

The fix? Make the button persistent and always visible. That single change reduced checkout drop-off by 14%.

The takeaway is simple: look at user behavior.

Where do people stop? What are they clicking? Where are they hesitating? Use tools like heatmaps, scroll depth tracking, or even session replays—not to chase vanity metrics, but to understand experience gaps. Every drop-off point is a chance to refine.

And when it comes to content, the same thinking applies. Look at your most visited blog posts or articles. Are they still accurate? Are they still converting? Updating a popular post with a stronger CTA, a better internal link, or a fresher reference can breathe new life into content you already have. It's not glamorous, but it's smart.

All of this boils down to one principle: test, don't guess.

You don't need to launch a perfect version of anything. You need to launch, learn, and iterate. If a section of your homepage isn't pulling its weight, test a variation. If people aren't scrolling past the fold, try moving something important higher up. If your email opt-in form isn't converting, rewrite the copy and test a different incentive.

Making smart changes isn't about perfection—it's about progress.

You won't get everything right on the first try, but if you keep improving the experience, piece by piece, your site will stay relevant, effective, and aligned with your goals.

And that's the point. You're not just building a website—you're running it. Nurturing it. Making it better, week by week.

It's not about having the most beautiful design or the trendiest layout. It's about making decisions that help real people move through your site more easily.

Smart changes, over time, build great websites.

Figure 6. The Iterative Improvement Cycle Diagram

This figure shows the four-step cycle you can use to continuously improve your website by turning insights into action and action into growth.

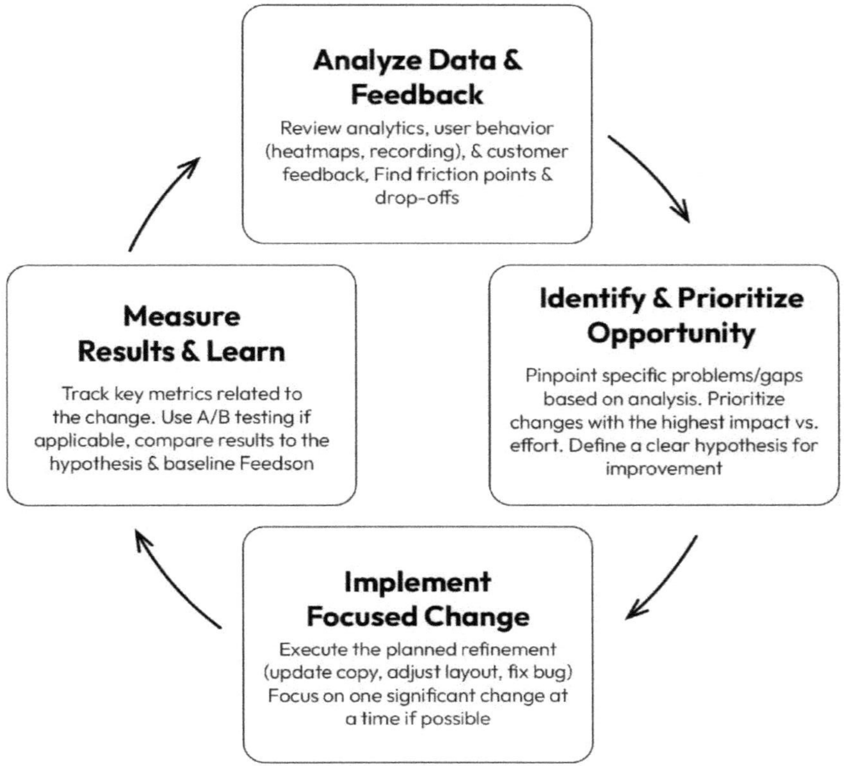

Know When It's Time for a Bigger Shift

Not every problem can be solved with a quick tweak. Sometimes the friction you're seeing isn't isolated—it's systemic.

That's when refinement stops being enough, and it's time to think bigger.

The challenge is knowing when you've crossed that line. It's easy to overreact to a dip in traffic or a disappointing quarter and blame the website. But just because performance has slipped doesn't mean you need to throw everything out.

Redesigns are expensive. They're disruptive. And if you do them for the wrong reasons, they can actually hurt more than help.

But if you've made thoughtful improvements—real ones, based on data—and things still feel off? That's when you step back and reassess the foundation.

A full redesign becomes the right move when the structure itself is misaligned with your business.

Maybe your offerings have changed dramatically, and your current site can't support the new narrative. Maybe your brand has matured, but your site still looks and sounds like it's built for startups. Maybe your users have shifted, and you're now attracting a completely different audience than you were two years ago.

Those are signals. They don't always show up in your analytics. Sometimes you feel them before you can measure them.

Your sales team says the site doesn't match the pitch anymore. Your prospects say they were confused by what they saw. Your competitors are outpacing you not because they're better, but because they're clearer.

Or maybe it's not even about business growth—it's about technical debt.

Your CMS is holding you back. Your content is a mess. You've stacked on so many plug-ins and workarounds that small changes take weeks. If your site is stopping you from executing, it's no longer an asset—it's a liability.

Outdated technology doesn't just slow your team down—it slows your users down, too. And that lag is often invisible to the people running the site. You're used to the quirks. You've learned the workarounds. But to a new visitor, those delays feel clunky and unprofessional.

Take mobile page performance, for example. When Google introduced AMP (Accelerated Mobile Pages), it wasn't just to reward faster load times—it was because users expected content to load instantly on their phones. AMP stripped out the bloat and forced sites to prioritize speed. While AMP isn't as central today as it once was, it raised the bar for what "fast" should feel like—especially on mobile.

Look at how newer platforms and tools are being built with speed and flexibility in mind. The best modern sites don't load everything at once. They load the right content at the right time. That means your visitor sees what matters first, without having to wait for the whole page to finish building in the background.

It's a smoother experience that just feels faster, even if the total load time hasn't changed. That kind of responsiveness sends a message: this brand is sharp, modern, and in control.

But it's not just about how fast the site loads—it's about how easy it is to evolve. When your tech stack is outdated or overly complex, small changes become big projects.

Teams work around the system instead of with it. You patch things up instead of solving the real problem. And over time, all those quick fixes start to show. Your homepage starts to feel like a patchwork of updates.

Another sign is when your team starts working around the site instead of with it. You launch landing pages on a separate platform because your site's too hard to update. You send people to PDFs because the site structure can't support certain content. You skip product pages because it's easier to send a direct link than to have people navigate.

That's not sustainable.

The best time to redesign is when your business has clearly evolved, and your site no longer reflects it.

When the changes you'd need to make aren't just surface-level—they're structural. When a clean slate would be faster, more efficient, and more effective than endlessly patching over cracks.

It's not a decision you make lightly. But when you do it for the right reasons, it's a powerful moment of alignment.

You're not just building a prettier version of the old thing. You're building a sharper, more strategic version of your business online.

That's what a real redesign should be: a reset that reflects where you are and where you're going.

Not a trend-driven facelift. Not a panic response. But a thoughtful evolution—a shift that makes everything clearer, faster, and more effective.

If your current site still works, keep refining. But if it's holding you back, be honest about it. Sometimes the smartest move is to stop patching and start fresh.

Future-Proofing Without Overbuilding

One of the biggest traps in web design is the desire to "build for the future."

It sounds smart. It feels strategic. But more often than not, it leads to a bloated website that tries to solve problems you don't have yet, at the expense of the experience your visitors need right now.

You see this all the time in redesign projects. Teams try to account for every possible campaign, every future use case, every hypothetical edge case.

They build overly complex content systems, layer in unnecessary functionality, and add page types that no one asked for. And in doing so, they create a site that's harder to manage, slower to update, and more confusing for visitors.

Future-proofing isn't about overbuilding. It's about building the right foundation—one that's flexible, not fragile.

That starts with structure.

If your navigation is clear, your page types are thoughtfully defined, and your CMS is set up to support your current content model, then you're already ahead.

You don't need to build ten landing page templates you haven't used yet. You need one or two that can stretch to fit most scenarios, with clear rules for what belongs on them.

It's the same with components. Don't try to build a system that anticipates every future layout. Build one that supports your core message, your most common use cases, and the ways your team actually works.

You're not designing for theoretical users. You're designing for your real audience and your real content. The more grounded you stay in that reality, the better your site will perform.

But future-proofing isn't just about what you build—it's also about what you avoid.

Avoid content sprawl. Avoid creating pages or sections that have no clear owner. Avoid launching new formats unless you're ready to maintain them.

The best-performing sites are usually the ones that are ruthlessly edited. Every page has a purpose. Every section earns its place. And when something's no longer relevant, it gets removed.

That takes discipline. But it pays off.

Because what you're really future-proofing against isn't change—it's chaos. You're building a site that can grow without falling apart. One that can stretch without losing shape.

There's also a mindset shift here. You don't need to predict the future. You need to make smart decisions in the present that keep your options open.

Use flexible layout blocks instead of fixed templates. Set up your CMS so non-technical users can make updates without breaking things. Build processes for adding, testing, and removing content without needing a full dev sprint.

These aren't glamorous features, but they make the difference between a site that gets stale and one that keeps evolving.

In other words, the future isn't something you build toward all at once. It's something your site is quietly preparing for, every time you make a smart, scalable choice.

So if you're thinking long term, don't build more. Build better. Strip things down to what actually works, and create space for change—not complexity.

Because the best way to future-proof your site is to make sure it's easy to keep improving.

Final Word:
Perfect Isn't the Goal

There's no such thing as *the* perfect website—but there is a set of principles you can follow to get a version that's perfect for your business, your goals, and your users right now.

A website that works—for your audience, your business, your goals, and your stage of growth.

That's the real point of this book. Not perfection for perfection's sake, but a site that earns trust, drives action, and grows with you.

Your site is not just a billboard or a brochure. It's not a place for fancy words and pretty layouts. It's a tool. A key part of how people experience your brand. And when it works, it works hard. It educates. It persuades. It converts. It helps.

But here's the thing: it's never truly "done."

The good thing is that you don't need to get everything right all at once. The best sites didn't start perfect. They were launched, tested, broken, refined, reshaped. They evolved. Because the businesses behind them evolved too.

The point is: progress beats perfection.

So don't wait until you've figured everything out. Start by defining your goal. Then audit your site through that lens. What's getting in the way? What's unclear, slow, or clunky? What feels off to your users whether they say it or not?

Start there. Fix one thing. Then fix another.

Keep listening. Keep iterating. Keep building a site that's not just beautiful—but useful. One that actually works.

And if you ever find yourself stuck, overwhelmed, or tempted to burn it all down and start fresh—just come back to this:

What's the job of this page?

If you can answer that clearly, everything else becomes simpler.

Strip away what doesn't help. Highlight what does. Fix one thing, then another. And keep listening—to your users, to your data, to your gut.

Refining your site over time helps your visitors, and it also tells Google you're serious about quality. That's a signal worth earning.

Because great websites aren't just built once. They're built over time.

Keep going. You're closer than you think.

About The Author

Rafael Romis is the founder and CEO of Weberous, an award-winning digital agency known for building websites that don't just look great but also convert. With over a decade of experience in UX, design, and digital strategy, Rafael has led projects for global brands, high-growth eCommerce companies, and purpose-driven organizations, turning underperforming websites into engines for growth.

What sets Rafael apart is his focus on the full picture: not just how a website looks but how it works, converts, and evolves. His expertise has been featured in publications like Forbes, Entrepreneur, HubSpot, and GoDaddy, among others—where he's shared insights on digital marketing, eCommerce strategy, and building websites that actually work.

In The Anatomy of the PERFECT Website, Rafael shares the same principles his team uses every day—giving readers a practical, behind-the-scenes look at what makes a website succeed in the real world.

www.ingramcontent.com/pod-product-compliance
Lightning Source LLC
LaVergne TN
LVHW050934210926
848482LV00013B/617